C000176284

'You have in your hands a book that ha
you discover "how to live a life that is m
a book about developing character, not
to influence others. The chapters are bi
and challenge you. Before you act you need to reflect and that's
what reading these daily doses of wisdom will help you to do. If you
genuinely want to live a better and larger life, read this book.'

    Professor Paul McGee, Sunday Times *Best-selling Author and
Motivational Speaker and Coach*

'Paul Hargreaves has a favourite interview question that few can
answer: "Which business leader do you admire?" There is clearly a
shortage of them. We badly need inspirational leaders, so Hargreaves
has written a book to address this gap. It is a 50-day plan to help the
aspiring leader reflect daily on the key practices that lead to great
leadership. Reassuringly practical, it sets out a programme for the
fourth bottom line of personal transformation. Love and service
are beguiling, and any leader who sets about freeing themselves
to engage with the humanity of those whom they lead will find
themselves richly rewarded.'

    Dr Eve Poole, Third Church Estates Commissioner and Author of
Leadersmithing

'This is an inspiring read and not for the faint-hearted. It helps open
our eyes to the very different landscape – business and everyday
– that is achievable if we become more self-aware by trying, with
the help of this book, to peel off the layers of conditioning we have
all acquired throughout our lives. This book offers up a personal
challenge to change, and if enough people take up that challenge we
will start to live in a better, more equal world.'

    Wilfred Emmanuel-Jones, Founder of The Black Farmer

'Having just watched the film *Dark Waters* which shows the ugly side
of leadership, this book is a brilliant shining light on the opposite:
what makes a great leader. With 50 easy-to-follow examples
interwoven with personal stories from the author, the novel idea is
to read through and reflect on one characteristic a day for 50 days,
which is a simple way to explore and make changes. In this way we
can become the leaders we want to be.'

    Mark Cuddigan, CEO Ella's Kitchen – Europe

'*The Fourth Bottom Line* is an essential read for 21st-century leaders, who recognise that there has been a paradigm shift in what is required by leaders today: the stagnated and historical perspectives held by leaders within the 20th century will no longer suffice and a new way of thinking is required. *The Fourth Bottom Line* navigates you through interesting stories about real people and gives you real insights from thought leaders. This book will reinvigorate and renew the way you think, the way you lead and the way that you interact with others in a more empathetic way, with the clear understanding that as leaders we are here to serve and success is determined by how well we serve others.'

Dr Carlton Brown PhD, MBA, PGDiP, F.APS, Business Growth Specialist

'"Self-acceptance is necessary before any change" – such a poignant line in Paul's book, and one that I feel is so important for all of us. Paul really has set leadership out in the most wonderful way, creating a book that is a guide and support for us to keep by our side. We can all lead when we realise what leadership really looks like; it's time for us to put humility first and only then will the meaning of leadership become truly valuable. Leadership is not just a title: it is something that comes from within and inspires others, because you are being uniquely you for the good of this world.'

Jules White, Chief Inspiration Officer – Live it, Love it, Sell it

'Paul quite rightly prefaces the book with an explanation that male does not equal masculine, and female is not the same as feminine. This is a concept I have realised few fully comprehend. Each of us has elements of both masculine and feminine. And the truth is that our experiential conditioning indicates that leaders are exclusively masculine in nature. This much-needed book explores the feminine, where can be found truly authentic leadership. If this could be taught on MBA courses, perhaps we would create a better world.'

Mike Jennings, Chairman of the Jennings Group, Author, TedX Speaker

'Paul Hargreaves has the uncanny skill of putting words to what others are thinking at just the right time. Both as a visionary, but also as a practical, genuine and approachable man, he yet again points the way to where leaders need to look and offers realistic solutions to the challenge of our generation.'

Daniel Yehuda Frohwein, Founder of www.realiseyourpotential.com

'This book needs to be on the bookshelf of all those aspiring leaders who want to take their businesses to the next level. A book that should be read, reread and reflected upon on a regular basis. The thought-provoking characteristics necessary for good leadership, being insightful and sapient, because Paul has a way of engaging with the reader that shows empathy with those who will be exemplars in any field of endeavour.'

> *Carole Spiers, FISMA FPSA MIHPE, Founder of International Stress Awareness Week*

'*The Fourth Bottom Line* adds a new dimension into leaders' lives – that is personal transformation of the leader themselves. Paul describes how the world desperately needs a new breed of modern-day, legendary leaders. Paul shows that to be a truly outstanding leader you need to work on yourself constantly while in the privileged position of being in the top job. This is a practical and transformational guide, taking you on a 50-day journey. Thoroughly recommended.'

> *Lloyd Wigglesworth, Partner, The Alexander Partnership*

In *The Fourth Bottom Line*, Paul Hargreaves reconnects us with the essence of leadership and offers a practical guide to nurture the inherent human qualities that make the difference between a leader we MUST follow and one we WANT to follow. This book takes you on a 50-day journey into the heart of your being. From there you will discover a more profound, and longer lasting, source of leadership than any formal position of authority could ever provide you with. I have seen first-hand Paul put into practice what he teaches and how, in the context of his own company, this not only leads to high level of staff engagement but also exceptional business results.

> *Mark Vandeneijnde, Co-Founder, Being at Full Potential*

'In his second book, *The Fourth Bottom Line*, Paul links his aim to create a better world through purpose-driven businesses, with a practical step-by-step roadmap for leaders everywhere to transform themselves. Paul drives action by highlighting 50 characteristics of next-practice leadership, as a '1-per-day' medicinal for leaders to take on board, road test and adopt going forward. A superb and most appropriate read for our times, with plenty of practical advice, action orientation and focus on the fourth bottom line.'

> *Jeremy Blain, Founder and CEO, Performance Works International*

'Paul recognises that the elevation in leadership quality needed at this critical point in history requires us to each embark upon an intense period of inner reflection. This book provides a valuable pathway for that essential journey – well done!'

Chris Cooper, Behavioural Strategist, Author, Business Elevation Show Host

'In his second book, Paul Hargreaves examines the motivation, method and mindset of being a more conscious leader, the characteristics, qualities, and attributes we can adopt, and offers a step-by-step, daily practice to bring more awareness to our lives. Paul shows us that we must go deep within to learn how to lead from love; when we love who we are, who we serve, what we create and why we create it, we will be leading from the heart and able to make a positive impact on everything and everyone around us. Follow Paul's 50-day practice, watch the magic unfold and be the leader, inspiration and guide that others want to follow.'

Stephen Karbaron, Business Transformation Consultant

'This book, like Paul himself, is above all thoughtful, thorough and accessible. Following up on looking at the bigger context for any 21st-century leadership in *Forces for Good*, Paul now delves into the deeper, personal motivation required to become adequate for this task. Challenging but never judgemental, inspirational but never impractical, here are definitions, quotes, insights and actions which can stimulate a fresh self-awareness. In our time of such disruptive social and cultural change, we are encouraged and enabled towards a recognition and embodiment of our deepest and best human values.'

Sue Mitchell, MSc., M. Assoc for Coaching, Organisational and Individual Wellbeing Coach

'Leadership begins deep inside us. If you want to create ripples of positive change, spend time with this book. Its inspiring stories, incisive questions and personal reflections by Paul Hargreaves will shift how you see yourself and your place in helping to heal the world.'

Sarah Rozenthuler CEO Bridgework, Psychologist and Author

The Fourth Bottom Line

Flourishing in the new era of compassionate leadership

PAUL HARGREAVES

The Fourth Bottom Line
Flourishing in the new era of compassionate leadership

ISBN 978-1-912300-32-7
eISBN 978-1-912300-33-4

Published in 2021 by SRA Books
© Paul Hargreaves 2021

Printed in the UK

The author would like to thank the following for permission to use copyright material: Lisa Cumming and Quakers in Britain for the extract from the blog post 'Experiencing the silent walk for Grenfell' (2018); Eve Poole for permission to quote from her blog post '7 Deadly Sins – capitalism's flat-earth problem and what to do about it' (29 January 2014) at evepoole.com; Sujith Ravindran for the extract from The Being Leader (YOU-Nity Project Academy, 2014); Richard Stengel and Penguin Random House for the extract from Mandela's Way by Richard Stengel (Crown, 2010); Akaya Windwood and the Interaction Institute for Social Change for the extract from the website article 'No More Experts' (IISC, 2013). While every effort has been made to trace all copyright holders, if any have been inadvertently overlooked, the author and publisher will be pleased to make the necessary arrangements at the first opportunity.

To all those leaders who have gone before us.
We stand on your shoulders.

Contents

Foreword

Sujith Ravindran

Founder, Global Foundation for BEING Leadership

'Very few people or companies can clearly articulate WHY they do WHAT they do. By WHY I mean your purpose, cause, or belief – WHY does your company exist? WHY do you get out of bed every morning? And WHY should anyone care?' says Simon Sinek in his acclaimed book, *Start with WHY*.

There are enough reasons to agree with Simon's statement.

For decades we have come to believe that people bought a company's product or services for their functional or emotional benefits. That has been true.

However, in the past decade and a half I have noticed a new trend emerging. People have started to question the values and conduct of the companies from which they buy. They demand to know the ingredients of the products they consume.

These days it is very normal for consumers to investigate the ecological footprint of the products they buy.

How much plastic is used? How many trees are cut? What emissions are released? These are normal questions raised by consumers to leaders today.

Consumers have also been taking a stand for social equity. Today it is normal for them to demand fair trade, fair pay, fair contribution to taxes and a commitment against child labour. They are big on honouring the origin of the things they consume. And they do not hesitate to call out leaders who do not take a favourable stand on these matters.

Annual general meetings are becoming courtrooms where leaders are held to account. When it comes to voting for an extension for management, character has become as important a criterion as performance is.

Millennials and women are at the forefront of this shift in consumer consciousness. When they take a product home, it is not unusual for them today to discuss the virtues of the company they buy from, and not just the virtues of the products they buy. They follow the news and browse the Internet to ascertain whether a certain product deserves their consideration or not.

A similar activism is today visible in the world of politics and governance too. Citizens are vocal against misgovernance, and they come down heavily on any inconsistencies in our democracies. They consider themselves stakeholders and custodians of human rights, whichever part of the world it may concern. Hashtags have become the voice of a generation of citizenry who expect the highest standards from our institutions and their leaders.

To our relief, many leaders have responded with great eagerness to this collective cry of humanity. The world over, I notice a generation of leaders who genuinely believe that good leadership comes from a deep inner place of luminous virtues. It is a refreshing sight to observe. Many leaders realise that it is not *what we know* that matters, it is *who we are*. Leadership development programs now emphasise the content of leadership as being as important as the technocracy of leadership.

Amid our intense self-enquiry around leadership virtues, something dramatic has happened to our world, laying a new context for leadership. The Covid-19 pandemic hit the globe. And that has changed the entire nature of the debate around leadership. Where leadership virtues were once a useful addition to great performance, they have now become an absolute necessity for our very survival.

Here is where Paul's work becomes important for leaders. Simon Sinek suggests that we start with WHY. Paul insists that we go a level deeper in our collective quest for co-evolution and focus on the WHO. What a great reminder!

In his first book, *Forces for Good*, Paul argued that (higher) purpose is quintessential for a world that works for everyone. In *The Fourth Bottom Line*, he goes to an amazing new depth and lays out a number of virtues that make up the DNA of the post-Covid leader.

This is a timely reminder for humanity. As I write this, we are just coming out of the Covid-related lockdown. And if there is one thing that the lockdown has proven to us, it is that the old 'normal' was not sustainable. How could it be?

Most people had completely neglected self-care and self-realisation. Work-life balance has been off, economic inequity had grown to its largest ever, political apathy and ideological polarisation has been intense, not to mention the ecological devastation we have been witnessing.

The lockdowns have given us the blessing of precious time to reimagine our future. And more than anything, we have been called to reimagine our leadership, both as individuals and as institutions. This book is a valuable almanac in that reimagination process.

I have come to recognise that the leaders of a VUCA[1] future must be holistic. In order for them to fulfil their sacred duty, leaders must embody all the five natures of leadership depending on the five levels of consciousness. They must be sages, statesmen, technocrats, magicians and commanders, depending on the call of the hour.

This integral nature of leadership is best encapsulated in these words of the mystics: *centred as a mountain in your **being**, flowing like a river in your **doing***. This paradox of two seemingly opposite energies exposes the secret of successful leadership in the VUCA world.

The above wisdom is the big reason why I have loved reading Paul's book. This book has felt like a leadership deck of cards where each chapter speaks directly to the very essence of our *being* and *doing*.

Leadership virtues such as being *compassionate*, *silent* and *non-judgmental* may seem synonymous with the sages and moral teachers from our mythology. However, aren't we being asked to transcend to that level of leadership to become the guides for humanity that feels lost and is on a quest to reconnect with its essence?

Being *forgiving*, *integrous* and *justice-loving* may seem important virtues for royalty and statesmen, but aren't the times asking us to be queen or king-like? If we do not attempt to model these virtues, who will give hope to our young ones and neighbours who are seeking to realise their own human potential?

Being *content*, *persevering* and *curious* are important leadership qualities of legendary experts and scholars. Yet in a world where the knowledge paradigm keeps shifting at light speed, are we not called to lead as technocratic leaders where asked? Who else will enlighten those in the dark and searching?

Being *collaborative*, *empathetic* and *friendly* might sound like virtues of caring family members. For a world that is divided and in disharmony, aren't we expected to become magicians who widen our notion of family and take these values outside our homes?

Being *courageous*, *protective* and *resilient* are qualities usually

---

1 'VUCA is an acronym – first used in 1987, drawing on the leadership theories of Warren Bennis and Burt Nanus – to describe or to reflect on the volatility, uncertainty, complexity and ambiguity of general conditions and situations.' (Wikipedia)

associated with the commanders who have led us through tumultuous times. That level of firmness may seem out of style for a world that is seeking reconciliation. Yet when we are faced with a human tribe that seems directionless and is in disarray, should we not awaken these qualities and own that mantle of commander?

This book is a valuable compilation of virtues that enable the realisation of all leadership types. Use this book to that end.

Before I close, let me share this very interesting observation.

Recently, the World Economic Forum came out with a very noble initiative called the Great Reset. The ambition of the program is to create markets and economies that are fair to everyone, invest in advancing equality and sustainability, and harness innovations to support the public good. All noble aspirations.

However, before the announcement hit the newsstand, the Great Reset got labelled as the Great Rip-off. It got spun into something totally opposite to what some leaders had hoped for.

> 'The Great Reset is about maintaining and empowering a corporate extraction machine...'

> 'The Great Reset will do nothing to help Mother Nature but will instead prop up and expand the very industrial capitalist system which is murdering her.'

Such is the level of faith deficit in most of the top leaders of today's establishment. Unfortunate.

For most of us, we have a life blessed with everything. There is enough wealth to go around. We have technology at our fingertips that has made the world smaller. Any person we love can be reached with one click. The global flow of goods has made it effortless for us to meet our every material need. Our health and wellbeing are taken care of by an army of caregivers.

If there is one thing that we could do more with: that is leadership that does right. Paul's book is a priceless key to manifest that ideal.

All these years I have known Paul, I have seen him living the virtues laid out in this book. Let us follow his example and start with ourselves. Let us start within.

Introduction

One of my favourite interview questions to ask is: 'Tell me which person has most inspired you in your adult life?' Occasionally the interviewee will give a really pleasing answer, such as an inspirational teacher at school or a previous manager who took them under their wing and nurtured them, but more often than not, they will mention a famous business leader (often the one living in the Virgin Islands) whom they have never met, and who therefore probably hasn't impacted their life very much. This saddens me, as this world desperately needs more leaders who can be looked up to and copied, not in terms of what they do, but in terms of their character. The fact that this interview question, which I must have asked well over 100 times, only has a 10 per cent rating on what I would call a good answer, proves that we need more inspiring leaders who, by their supreme example, can pass on their life experience to others.

The fourth bottom line

My first book, *Forces for Good*, was written to inspire business leaders to lead their businesses in such a way as to make a positive difference for good in the world, based around the 'people, planet, profit' motif. Yet even in the process of writing it, I realised that I couldn't continue to make outward positive differences without making internal changes of my own and increasing my ability to love others. This is what I called the fourth bottom line and the area about which I have been asked to speak the most since the publication of *Forces for Good*. Many successful 21st-century businesses are now looking towards the triple bottom line, rather than the old-school single financial bottom line. However, these businesses of a new compassionate capitalism need a new type of leader who makes decisions based on love; and it is embedding this empathy within ourselves that I called the fourth bottom line, without which we will not see a healed planet and greater equality in the world.

Indeed, without the character development of leaders, any positive changes we make may not be long lasting, as various pressures and difficulties are bound to come. For permanent change in the 21st century's businesses, politics, social enterprises and charities, we need more inspirational leaders with greater depth of character. Their way of living, both in private and public, will be contagious and inspire a new generation of leaders who in turn will help reverse the many injustices in the world as well as quicken the work to reverse climate change. Today's very unequal and unfair world desperately needs those leaders who put others first rather than themselves, and who will find, perhaps surprisingly, that they become happier themselves as a result.

Too often, we have been given the wrong view of leadership. Too many people, including leaders themselves, aspire to be lauded by others, gather obscene amounts of material possessions and operate in power rather than humility. Some leaders have operated from their own fears, insecurities or irrationalities, which has made it difficult for them to truly serve the people they are leading or become the humble and vulnerable leaders their people need them to be. Many leaders in the developed world have learned neoliberalist, capitalist values from their schools, parents and universities from within an extreme capitalist system that is now crumbling around them, and whose death throes became more obvious to many during the Covid-19 pandemic in 2020. Part of becoming an inspiring leader is to unlearn some of what society has taught us; throughout this book, I will refer to these wrong values as being part of our 'conditioned self'.

Conditioned or unconditioned self?

Many people operate from their conditioned self for the majority, if not all, of their lives. The conditioned self is driven by beliefs developed through our experiences during childhood and adulthood, and through wider cultural and social influences. The hurt and pain we have experienced in our past forms our behaviour in the present. Maintaining our self-image becomes the most important thing to us and our reflex responses often fall short of our best selves, which others need us to be. We perceive that our behaviour is normal when we are viewing normality through the rather narrow telescopic lens of a Western upbringing and culture. We not only need to throw off much of our personal conditioning, but also our cultural and educational conditioning if we are to become self-aware leaders who are free from a faulty self-image; in other words, it means moving towards operating from what we will call our 'unconditioned selves'.

As far as models of leadership are concerned, our conditioning is equally well ingrained. For all our lives, and for millennia before, most leaders have been men, and most of them have been unbalanced as far as valuing the masculine and feminine are concerned. Those men have operated too much from the macho, competitive side of themselves and haven't been free enough to allow the feminine to shine through. As a result, many of the women in leadership, not through their own fault, have had to give pre-eminence to the masculine too. Men – we have a lot to answer for! We absolutely need many more female leaders, and probably at this time we need more of them than men, to help redress the balance. We also need more balanced men, who know the feminine and give her space both externally and internally. Many of the characteristics we will look at in this book would have traditionally been known as feminine qualities.

We can always learn much from other cultures, which helps us realise that a lot of what we consider normal is not normal elsewhere; and people in developing cultures frequently have much more to teach us about good character than anything we Westerners can bring to them. I have often travelled to Asia and Africa and I always come back challenged, humbled and inspired to live life in a way that is more beneficial to others. It is no coincidence that more people within the business, social enterprise and political worlds in the West are embracing Eastern practices such as mindfulness, meditation and yoga than ever before.

Who is this book for?

This book is for those of us who want to operate at a purer level of humanity; those individuals who have moved through pain from their past, through a negative self-image, and who have transcended the negatives within their own culture to be the best they can be for the world. It is for those people who have seen that there is a higher plane on which to live; a place where they can have more positive influence on others through channelling more of the good that is within them. Yes, they still have days when they are operating from their unconditioned or egoistical self, but they learn to move quickly out of that old mode of being into greater self-awareness.

The characteristics we will explore in this book are aspirational for anyone who is excited about a new, purer form of leadership, which they may have glimpsed previously in figures such as Mother Teresa,

Martin Luther King, Nelson Mandela and Mahatma Gandhi. These are all individuals whom very few of us today have met, but the stories of their leadership and the impact they've had are now the stuff of legend. We live in a world that is just as unequal and as full of injustice as that in which those legends lived, some would perhaps say even more so. We certainly live on a planet that has been degraded to a huge extent within the past 50 years and which needs modern-day legendary leaders to inspire the solutions.

The book is not for those people who simply want to tackle an intellectual exercise – as they would be sorely disappointed anyway! – but it is for those of us who enjoy seeing ourselves change for better. That is not to say you need to beat yourself up as you go through it; that would be the last thing I would want. Self-acceptance is necessary before any change, and it is not a paradox to accept ourselves and know we are OK as we are yet still be inspired to become more compassionate, thankful, inclusive and the other desirable traits of modern leadership that we are going to be examining within these pages.

How to use this book

I have found the practice of being still for 30 minutes or so in the morning helps me have a better, more productive day; and I would thoroughly recommend this practice to you too if you do not do this already. Depending on your work or family situation, you may find it better to take some moments in the evening, or perhaps find a short 'timeout' during your working day. I would recommend you start with a short meditation (there are plenty of apps available for this), and I would also encourage you to use a notebook or journal. This is useful for noting down any thoughts or actions that come up; also, before spending time in quiet, it is great to write down any distracting thoughts about the things you need to do that day, which may get in the way of this moment of calm.

In your moment of reflection, turn to the chapters in this book. The chapters are designed to be read one per day, and you may perhaps want to read them twice, at different times during the course of that day, to aid with your reflections and help the lessons and questions sink in. There are 50 chapters in total and as psychologists say it takes 45 days to change behaviour patterns, if you are not used to sitting still and reflecting every day, you may have ingrained the habit by the end of this book. The words we are looking at each day are adjectives to stimulate the thought: 'Could I be described as a self-aware (Day 1), humble (Day 2), forgiving (Day 3)… type of person or leader?' If yes, then great, you can always become more so; if no, then don't worry – we all have strengths and weaknesses, and we can work on addressing our many shortcomings.

For each day and chapter, there is a dictionary definition. I have varied which dictionaries these come from, choosing the definition that conveys most closely the heart of the characteristic I am trying to describe. You may want to repeat the definition to yourself once or twice to let its meaning sink in. There follow four quotes each day from some exceptional individuals, and you may wish to reflect on these for a few moments as they often express a slightly different aspect of the characteristic we are examining. The main chapter content takes the form of a four- to five-minute read, exploring the day's characteristic through the stories and experiences of myself and others. Finally, I suggest three actions, some of which are intended for reflection in the moment and about which you can make notes in your journal; and there is also usually an action or two to put into practice during the rest of your day. I suggest you allow at least seven minutes for this section, which means that each chapter should take around 12 to 15 minutes in total each day, perhaps following a 10-minute meditation if that is your usual practice – but there are, of course, no rules. Please use the book in the way that works best for you.

Characteristics of leadership

The list of characteristics and attributes described in this book is by no means exhaustive, but has been formed from observing great leaders from the past and present who truly inspire and love others, and who have made a massive, positive difference to the world in which they lived or live. It is often by looking up to those we admire that we are called to follow their inspiring example; and this has certainly been the case for me when I read about the moral giants from our past and present. I remain painfully aware of my own shortcomings daily – as my family and work colleagues would be able to tell you! Clearly, this book is not exclusively written for leaders, although if you attain depth in even a few of the human qualities we will be studying, then others will be inspired and follow you – and that makes you a leader. Many people who do not call themselves leaders have more people following them than those who give themselves the title!

The chapters are structured in no particular order of priority and there is no gradation of difficulty. Every person reading them will be more developed in certain areas than others, and you may feel the need to work more on some areas than others. No one will ever be perfect, but as we journey through our lives and learn from our experiences, I do believe that each day we can become more whole and more loving to others. Growing in one or many more of these qualities will help you to inspire, move and help others, and as a result the world will be a better place. That is my hope and dream, as we start with Day 1...

DAY 1 » **Self-aware**

Dictionary definition:

> 'Conscious of one's own feelings, character, etc.'
> *Collins English Dictionary*

Quotes:

> 'Of all deceivers fear most yourself!'
> *Søren Kierkegaard, Danish philosopher*

> 'Everything that irritates us about others can lead us to an understanding of ourselves.'
> *Carl Jung, Swiss psychoanalyst*

> 'Self-awareness is our capacity to stand apart from ourselves and examine our thinking, our motives, our history, our scripts, our actions, and our habits and tendencies.'
> *Stephen Covey, American educator and businessperson*

> 'Self-awareness is not self-centeredness, and spirituality is not narcissism. "Know thyself" is not a narcissistic pursuit.'
> *Marianne Williamson, American politician and activist*

Insights

There's a good reason we are looking at self-awareness first on our journey to better leadership. I would go as far as to say that without increasing our self-awareness, there is little hope for the top leaders that this world desperately needs. In a podcast with Tim Ferriss in February 2020, Brené Brown claimed that 'the reason there's so much hate and unhappiness in the world is because people lack self-awareness.' I tend to agree and if we think back to the poor leadership that we may have had the misfortune to experience in our own lives, there's a very good chance that low or no self-awareness is a common factor. As I write, I am thinking of a particular person I used to know, who had absolutely no clue about how he impacted those around him, nor the trail of destruction he left behind; and when he was confronted about the upset he had caused, he simply told people they should grow a thicker skin.

In her book *Insight: The Power of Self-Awareness in a Self-Deluded World*, Tasha Eurich draws on years of research to suggest that up to 95 per cent of people believe that they are reasonably self-aware, but only 10 to 15 per cent of people actually are. Now, let's be clear that self-awareness is very different to being self-absorbed, a state which social media has helped increase to international pandemic levels. Self-awareness occurs on two levels. First, it means having an accurate view of our strengths and weaknesses, knowing what makes us tick, what makes us happy or sad and being aware of when our behaviour could be better and knowing some of the reasons for that conditioned behaviour. Second, it is about having a realistic view of how we connect with the outside world and the impact we make there on other people.

So, in summary, there are those who have never considered whether or not they are self-aware – and they are probably not reading this book. Of those who do consider themselves to be self-aware, most are not. There are two levels on which they may not be: internal and external. Let's not be too down on ourselves, though. There's a good chance that, if you are reading this book, you are aware of areas of yourself and your leadership that could be better, and you may have been attracted to reading it by recognising that some of the chapter titles relate to areas in which you know you can improve, so you are probably well on your way.

With respect to the second, external form of self-awareness, I had a rude awakening about this as a teenager, which certainly helped me lose any delusions of grandeur I may have had at the time. I was seventeen and at a youth group event where, for some reason, the leader of the group decided to run a 'clear the air' exercise. We were asked to look around the room and ask ourselves whether we had an issue with anyone else there; then, on his signal, to go and talk to them about it. The bell sounded and I was talking to the first person in front of me, when I looked up and saw there was a queue behind them, while the rest of the room was relatively empty! At that moment, my previously unaware teenage self realised the impact I was having on others, which hopefully had a positive effect on me in later years. I certainly reflected for a while afterwards about what people had said to me and learned from it. And that, in a nutshell, is the key to growing in self-awareness. It is not about narcissistic introspection but detaching ourselves from incidents and conversations, and taking an objective view on events or what has been said, and then learning from this. *Why did I feel like that? What could I do differently next time?* It is about moving forward and not standing still.

I can't think of a better example of someone growing into self-aware-ness than Terry Waite, who, while negotiating for the release of hostages in 1987 as the Archbishop of Canterbury's envoy, was taken into captivity himself for nearly five years, the first four of which were in solitary confinement. Very few human beings have four years in which to get to know themselves as thoroughly as he did, and as a result I recommend reading anything Terry has written, for it all shows great self-aware-ness. Here is an extract from *Footfalls in Memory* (1996), written after his release, about an experience he had as a young man:

> I was quite terrified at the prospect of revealing my most private failings before another but took courage and did so. It was a small but important step in my life. One of the reasons this step had significance was that I began to learn what great capacity I, in company with most human beings, have for self-deception. Objective comments, be they from confessor, therapist, or friend, seem to be to be vital if one would grow up. They are rarely easy to accept.

Let's look now at a fictional example from the world of business to help us understand self-awareness in a little more detail. A company director of a growing business, let's call her Helen, has a great team, but taking the business to the next level involves a level of financial risk that she hasn't been exposed to previously. Helen is reluctant to take that risk, despite several other board members and the bank being very keen. In fact, when they talk about the potential debt involved, she starts to feel nauseous and light-headed, and on one occasion she has to leave the room during discussions. As Helen is the main shareholder, the organisation delays taking the next step and now, a few months later, the business is stagnating. As she has a level of self-awareness, Helen knows in her heart that she has an issue with financial risk and she engages with a coach, who starts to help her explore her feelings of anxiety about money. They stem from Helen having an alcoholic father who regularly gambled the money needed to buy the family food or school uniforms. A fear of being in debt and not having enough money for food and clothes is buried in Helen's psyche, so that now, despite being relatively affluent, those fears are still present for her. Stepping further into her self-awareness will mean Helen acknowledging she has a weakness in this area and trusting others to make wise decisions around financial risk while stopping herself from blocking them.

We all experience some levels of trauma, pain or upset as children, which can leave us fearful or vulnerable. As we grow older, we create barriers around these vulnerable areas to protect ourselves. These defence mechanisms can create certain behaviours around those fears which subsequently bury the roots of the fear and insecurity even deeper as we become well practised at getting through life with our coping mechanisms or masks in place. Growing in self-awareness is about becoming aware of these blind-spots or realising that our version of 'normal' might look very different from the 'normal' of most of the population.

So, how do we grow in self-awareness? First, by spending time reflecting on our values, character and various aspects of our life, as we will be doing in each chapter of this book. In one of the quotes at the start of this chapter, Stephen Covey talks about the ability to stand back and look at ourselves from the outside; if you wish, read it again now. Second, by learning to connect with our inner feelings and understand why we feel the way we do. If our emotions are provoked during a conversation, it's helpful to learn to pause before we reply, so we can gain more insight into ourselves. Third, by asking for constructive feedback from others, which will help reveal our blind-spots and help us understand that others sometimes view a problem in a completely different, and often better, way than we do. Finally, we can learn to accept ourselves as a unique individual complete with our own suffering, fears and weakness. We admit to ourselves that we will never be perfect and that we will always be learning and inspired to change by those who are different to us. This is incredibly exciting – and the starting point of being a leader with self-awareness.

Actions

Learning to be self-aware today:

» Reflect for a few moments on how well you know yourself. How easy do you find it to stop your active mind and simply reflect on who you are? Journal any thoughts that arise.

» Think back to the last time you felt anger or upset at the words or actions of another. Are you aware of why you felt that way?

» Ask someone else today what your strengths and weaknesses are. This may be difficult, and you may need to give them some warning, but I promise it will be rewarding and will help you grow in self-awareness.

DAY 2 » **Humble**

Dictionary definition:

'Marked by meekness or modesty in behaviour, attitude, or spirit; not arrogant or prideful.'
Free Dictionary

Quotes:

'Humility is not thinking less of yourself, it's thinking of yourself less.'
C. S. Lewis, British writer and theologian

'It would be very egotistical of me to say how I would like to be remembered. I'd leave that entirely to South Africans. I would just like a simple stone on which is written "Mandela".'
Nelson Mandela, South African anti-apartheid revolutionary

'Humility is like underwear; essential, but indecent if it shows.'
Helen Nielsen, American script writer

'Humility is throwing oneself away in complete concentration on something or someone else.'
Madeleine L'Engle, American author

Insights

Mahatma Gandhi was surely one of the humblest people who ever lived. He was the embodiment of humility itself and took inspiration from many ancient sages and mystics, both from within India and beyond. I was slightly surprised on reading his autobiography to discover that he was also inspired by another mystic called Jesus, so much so that he apparently considered becoming a Christian when living in South Africa. Unfortunately, when he tried to visit a local church, he was refused entrance due to the colour of his skin. (This not surprising to learn, in light of what we know of the endemic racism in that country, but still shocking to hear that churches were as racist as the surrounding community, despite the example of their Great Teacher.)

Gandhi frequently used to serve the tea at his gatherings, something that a person of his social status would not normally do in the culture he belonged to. In fact, the orderlies, who were meant to serve, had to be convinced that Gandhi was only serving because it needed to be done and not because they were doing it wrong in some way. In Sujith Ravindran's excellent book *The Being Leader* (2014) we read more about the humility of this man:

> In another demonstration of humility, Gandhi was visiting a city to give a lecture to an organization he supported. Yet none of them knew what he looked like, so when he arrived, no one recognised him. He entered their building, and amidst the last-minute chaos of people preparing for the event, he noticed that a certain area of the floor needed sweeping. And when they finally realised who he was, they asked him, dumbfounded, 'Why are you doing such a menial task?'
>
> Gandhi replied, 'Because it needed to be done.'

That reply sums up a lot for me about the definition of humility. Gandhi simply didn't think in the same way that many of us do. Imagining myself in a similar situation, I would be thinking something like, 'Well, I know I shouldn't be doing this task, but if I am speaking in a dirty room, it won't reflect well on me, so I had better do it!' Or, 'I shouldn't be doing this, but it needs doing' – and then I'd remain resentful that I had had to pick up a broom when I was the speaker. My kind of reaction is the opposite of humility, not 'thinking of myself less' as C. S. Lewis puts it or, in other words, self-importance. Gandhi simply didn't think of himself as any different, better or more important than others. The job needed doing, he wasn't doing anything else, so he picked up the broom because it needed to be done.

There is another story of Gandhi travelling on a train to an event in another city. As you may know, Gandhi always insisted on buying a third-class ticket, rather than the first-class ticket that someone of his social status would normally buy. Not knowing who Gandhi was, another passenger going to the same event lay down on the wooden bench next to him on the train, where he took up most of the available space and even used Gandhi as a pillow, with his head on his lap. Gandhi didn't ask him to move all night, but sat in silence, probably not sleeping very much. When they arrived at their destination station and there were crowds of thousands of people there to greet Gandhi, the other passenger had to eat a large slice of humble pie and begged for Gandhi's forgiveness. If he had eaten some of that pie before the journey, he would have been less embarrassed on arrival.

Refusing to accept thanks and praise for something we have done is not being humble. In fact, the quick deflection of compliments is often disguised pride, and involves secretly wanting to be noticed and praised. This is commonly called false humility. True humility is accepting that we have done something good, but knowing that the power and strength to have done it come from outside ourselves and we are fortunate to be able to be in a place where we can do such things. Being pleased that something has gone well but not thinking that you are better than others because of it, is not a contradiction – especially if you know that many others could have done an equally good job. Not thinking of yourself as being better than others can be difficult if you have achieved success in business or life, but you will be respected and looked up to far more if you are genuinely humble.

In *Mere Christianity*, C. S. Lewis talks about a person with true humility being one who takes a genuine interest in other people. Too many of us are far too eager to talk about ourselves and too full of our own self-importance to listen properly to others and make them feel important. Could it be that true humility is reflected in an excitement at another's achievements? Does it entail celebrating and supporting their successes rather than our own? If so, many of us still have a way to go – judging by what I see every day on social media.

I haven't met very many famous people, but from my own and other's observations from encountering them at various events, they seem to fall into two types: those who are just going through the motions as part of their ongoing PR exercise and then a smaller number who amaze their fans by being extraordinarily generous with their time and conversation, and who seem to take a genuine interest in them. The latter type is more likely to be aware of their own shortcomings and less likely to be thinking that they are better than those they are meeting.

We may or may not be the kind of person whom others look up to, but that's not relevant when it comes to being humble or not. It is perhaps easier for those who are in some sort of leadership position to be more caught up in a sense of importance – which is why it is all the more important for leaders to be aware of and practise humility. And this is perhaps the difficulty with this characteristic: how on earth can we practise humility or assess how humble we are? While we can ask others whether we are patient or kind, for example, asking others whether we are humble is ridiculous, for, as we read earlier: 'Humility is like underwear; essential, but indecent if it shows.' Only we know whether we are wearing underwear, and only by self-examination can we rid ourselves of pride – the opposite of humility.

Actions

To practise humility today, first:

» Remind yourself now how small and insignificant you are on a global scale and how privileged you are to be here right now, wherever that is.

» Reflect for a minute or two on one of the truly great and humble leaders that you admire, or a humble leader you have met and how little they felt the need to talk about themselves.

» Make a conscious effort to truly listen to others and take a genuine interest in those you meet today. While you are talking to them, remind yourself of everything they do better than you.

DAY 3 » **Forgiving**

Dictionary definition:

'Able to grant pardon for a remission of (an offense, debt, etc.); absolve.'
Dictionary.com

Quotes:

'When you hold resentment toward another, you are bound to that person or condition by an emotional link that is stronger than steel. Forgiveness is the only way to dissolve that link and get free.'
Catherine Ponder, American minister

'To forgive is to set a prisoner free and discover that the prisoner was you.'
Lewis B. Smedes, American author and ethicist

'He who is weak can never forgive. Forgiveness is the attribute of the strong.'
Mahatma Gandhi, Indian political ethicist

'Whatever our religion, we know that if we really want to love, we must first learn to forgive before anything else.'
Mother Teresa, Albanian-Indian missionary

Insights

I am indebted to Richard Stengel, author and friend of Nelson Mandela, for his behind-the-scenes look at the great man. In his book *Mandela's Way*, Stengel relates:

> It is extraordinary that a man who was ill-treated for most of his life can see so much good in others. In fact, it is sometimes frustrating to talk with him because he almost never had a bad word to say about anyone. He would not even say a disapproving word about the man who tried to have him hanged. I once asked him about John Vorster, the Nazi sympathizing president of South Africa who tightened Apartheid and rued the fact that Mandela and his comrades have not been executed. 'He was a very decent chap,' Mandela said with complete sincerity. 'In the first place, he was very polite. In referring to us he would use courteous terminology.'

On another occasion mentioned in Mandela's own autobiography, *Long Walk to Freedom*, he describes an oppressive prison commander, who had given Mandela and his colleagues hell during his reign of terror on Robben Island. Mandela says of him:

> No one is born prejudiced or racist. No man is evil at heart. Evil is something instilled in or taught to men by circumstances, their environment or their upbringing. It is not innate. Apartheid made men evil, evil did not create Apartheid.

In my opinion, those last few sentences hold the clue to forgiveness. Being a forgiving person is to believe that there is good within everyone. Yes, they may have committed appalling acts, but there is a deposit of good, no matter how small, within everyone. Both loving your enemy and forgiving them will allow that good at least a chance of being revealed. You might possibly now be thinking of a particular person who either hurt you or committed appalling acts against your family, and you may be struggling with the whole idea of forgiving someone like that.

Let's reflect for a minute on the Catherine Ponder quote we considered earlier: 'Forgiveness is the only way to dissolve that link and get free.' Many of us intuitively know that holding on to a grievance is not doing us any good at all, yet we don't know where to start. I know I have experienced several occasions when my own lack of forgiveness of a parent or partner has resulted in those emotional chains stopping either party from moving forward. I think this is a common experience for us all. Forgiving people does not in any way condone what they have done, nor mean that they don't need to live with the consequences of their actions, but it releases something in us, which if not released will forever hold us back.

A friend shared with me the story of a man whose wife had an affair, and who then came to her senses and realised it was a huge mistake. She asked forgiveness of her husband, who forgave her and welcomed her back. The wife later discovered she was pregnant and when the baby was born it was clear from its skin colour that her husband wasn't the father. Yet he accepted the child and brought her up as his own. I find this story incredibly challenging and can think of all sorts of great reasons not to forgive if I were the husband in this scenario, yet he chose the way of forgiveness. We have all heard of extraordinary tales of parents forgiving the murderers of their own child, and we think to ourselves, how can they possibly do that? It must be incredibly difficult, but the truth is that a lack of forgiveness and resentment will eat us up, and while forgiveness can seemingly be impossible for acts of evil and both incredibly painful and challenging, it is what is best for us, and the only act that allows us to move forward.

Now, we have been talking about extraordinarily major acts of forgiveness, but it is also true that small daily resentments of people within our households and workplaces can have a similar, albeit smaller, impact. Even if subconscious, holding on to a grudge sends out subliminal messages to others that you don't care for them and don't accept them. We don't know neurologically or otherwise how this transmits itself to others, but whether it is through tiny changes in body language or facial expressions, believe me, people can pick up whether you have forgiven them or not. So, let's be determined to do something about it and walk through our lives without holding on to our grievances. Start with the small stuff and move on to the larger stuff, but we will be happier and more fulfilled people without the clutter of our grudges.

While there are links between all the characteristics or attributes within this book, there is possibly a closer link between forgiveness and inner contentment and indeed joy than some of the other character-istics we will be looking at. Forgiving others is a joyful experience both for the other party and for us, and can bring a tremendous sense of contentment and relief to all involved.

Actions

Here is the practice for today, but a good discipline for all days:

» Is there anyone you are going to meet today that you feel any resentment to, small or large? Actively forgive them now. Even if you don't feel like it, say the words as if they were in the room now. This practice may seem slightly weird if you haven't done anything like it before, but it works, believe me. The feelings may come later, or they may not, but actively continue to forgive them anyway.

» Is there anyone, dead or alive, from your past whom you are aware that you haven't forgiven? Imagine they are with you now and express words of forgiveness.

» Looking at it from the other angle, is there anyone you know who holds a grudge against you? Are you able to bring this into the conversation sensitively and encourage them in the practice of forgiveness? If you aren't going to meet them today, look for other opportunities to do this.

DAY 4 » **Empathetic**

Dictionary definition:

'Of, relating to, or characterized by empathy, the psychological identification with the feelings, thoughts, or attitudes of others.'
Dictionary.com

Quotes:

'Cultivate a sense of empathy – to put yourself in other people's shoes – to see the world from their eyes. Empathy is a quality of character that can change the world.'
Barack Obama, former president of the United States

'Leadership is about empathy. It is about having the ability to relate to and connect with people for the purpose of inspiring and empowering their lives.'
Oprah Winfrey, American talk show host

'I think we all have empathy. We may not have enough courage to display it.'
Maya Angelou, American poet and civil rights activist

'Empathy is about finding echoes of another person in yourself.'
Mohsin Hamid, British Pakistani novelist and brand consultant

Insights

The word 'empathy' comes from the Greek *empatheia – em* (into) and *pathos* (feeling), suggesting a movement towards and into someone else's pain, moving from one place, ourselves, to another place – the other's space, feelings and pain. If we have been led by great leaders in the past and have an emotional response when remembering them, it is likely that they were leaders with high empathy and that's the reason why we felt a connection with them. If we want to be inspirational leaders, then we also need to develop empathy, or to put it more accurately, nurture the empathy within us, which is more repressed in some people than others – as I am sure you have noticed.

Generally, those individuals who are more emotionally free themselves are able to feel the pain, suffering and desires of others. In Western culture, men tend to suppress their emotions more than women and may therefore need to work harder on developing their empathy than women. Just as, say, competitiveness is often viewed as a more masculine quality, empathy is definitely seen to be a more feminine one; that, of course, is not to say that women can leave all the competing to the men in their leadership teams and nor can men leave all the empathy to the women. Hopefully, we are all inspired to develop all these leadership qualities in balance.

I've found it interesting to look at two events that made global news headlines and which occurred in countries with female prime ministers at the time, but where there was a complete difference in the way that empathy was expressed: in one, very little empathy was shown and in the other, an extraordinary amount. The first example took place in 2017 when a terrible fire in a tower block in West London exposed Theresa May as someone who had very little emotional connection with the local residents, who had suffered terribly. The day after the Grenfell Tower fire, Theresa May visited the site but stood apart with the firefighters and her security guards, and extraordinarily did not ask to meet the locals. (Even if she had no empathy, surely this would have been a good PR move – if only to show people she was on their side.) She later regretted her action because she was criticised by others and admitted she had made a huge mistake, saying: 'But the residents of Grenfell Tower needed to know that those in power recognised and understood their despair. And I will always regret that by not meeting them that day, it seemed as though I didn't care.' I would suggest that while in a cerebral sense May knew she should care, she hadn't over the years developed the degree of empathy that meant her natural reaction to others' suffering would be to comfort them. Empathy would have put that reaction first and all other reactions well down the list.

Contrast that with what happened two years later, when Jacinda Ardern, the New Zealand prime minister, hugged and comforted Muslim men and women after the Christchurch shootings while identifying with them by wearing the hijab. The fact that this created so many newspaper headlines across the world, all describing how amazing it was that a leader could show so much empathy, indicates just how low the bar is. It troubles me that her response is so unusual for leaders of state. However, her leadership was not just about symbolic empathetic gestures; she later asked the bereaved for advice on the next steps for her government, involving them in the process beyond the immediate tragedy. Ardern's leadership was tested again in 2020 during the coronavirus pandemic, when New Zealand had one of the lowest death rates in the world due to a very early lockdown, once again showing her empathy followed by swift action. In fact, countries with leaders generally acknowledged as having empathetic leadership, including Canada and Ireland, have had far lower death rates than countries generally acknowledged to have leaders with little empathy, such as the UK, USA and Brazil. I don't think that is a coincidence.

However, the truth – that empathy is essential to good leadership – is not just subjective conjecture: there is good scientific evidence that empathy in the workplace is essential for those developing successful companies and organisations. In a 2007 paper, Gentry, Weber and Sadri analysed data from 6,731 managers from 38 different countries and found that empathy is positively related to job performance and is more important in some cultures than others. Managers who showed more empathy towards their direct reports are viewed as better performers in their job by their bosses. And the performance improvements demonstrated by greater empathy were more significant in cultures with greater power distance, i.e. more hierarchical cultures. Interestingly, the comparison the authors use in a graph in the study is between Columbia (low power-distance culture) and New Zealand (high power distance), indicating that Jacinda Ardern's empathy has more impact in New Zealand than it would do in Columbia. They conclude the study by saying:

> This study found that the ability to understand what others are feeling is a skill that clearly contributes to effective leadership. In some cultures, the connection between empathy and performance is particularly striking, placing an even greater value on empathy as a leadership skill.

The good news for those of us who didn't develop much empathy as children is that it can be learned as an adult leader, or preferably before you become a leader. I came to understand the importance of empathy later in my leadership journey, but how I wish I had understood this earlier. So, how do we grow in empathy? First, it is about slowing down and not purely focusing on the goal or cause, but on the people who are going to take you there. Many entrepreneurs are very goal-focused and sometimes lose touch with the feelings of their people. So slowing down and taking time to actively listen is vital, and I mean really listening which means turning your phone off. Second, encouraging other managers to show empathy is important and sitting in a room together not 'being productive' is perfectly OK in order to connect properly with your team members. Third, it is also important to learn to hear the meaning behind people's words, who may not always directly say what they are feeling. Finally, increasing our ability to put ourselves in other people's shoes by reflection and meditation will make us better leaders, as those people will feel respected, listened to, trusted and safe.

Empathy is in short supply these days, as more meetings and relationships happen through screens rather than face to face. Those leaders who can embrace empathy will not only be the more successful leaders but also those who, in Barack Obama's words, 'can change the world'.

Actions

Today, let's learn to walk in other people's shoes in empathy:

» How empathic are you as a person? Do you feel what others feel? Do you connect with others in the way that you lead? Reflect on those three questions and journal anything that comes to mind.

» When anything bad happens are our first thoughts for the goal being missed or for the people involved? Today, even if something small goes wrong, ask the person how they feel about it.

» Personally, I have found that my empathy has increased when I have been involved with people far less fortunate than me. There are lots of ways to volunteer or help in the community. Think about what you could do in this area.

DAY 5 » **Gracious**

Dictionary definition:

'Characterised by or showing kindness and courtesy.'
Free Dictionary

Quotes:

'If a man be gracious and courteous to strangers, it shows he is a citizen of the world.'
Francis Bacon, English philosopher and statesman

'I think sometimes it is more important to be gracious than to win.'
Dorothy Kilgallen, American journalist

'But what we can do, as flawed as we are, is still see God in other people, and do our best to help them find their own grace. That's what I strive to do, that's what I pray to do every day.'
Barack Obama, former president of the United States

'Be pretty if you can, be witty if you must, but be gracious if it kills you.'
Elsie de Wolfe, American actress

Insights

It was around ten years after the Falklands War between Argentina and Great Britain, and I was on a trip to Argentina, where part of our team's purpose was to see reconciliation and forge stronger relationships between the two countries. One day, we found ourselves on the top floor of a church hall-type building where we were to be served a meal; the rather humble environment perhaps added to the impact this event had on me. Never had I been on the receiving end of such gracious behaviour. We were served the food by our hosts with great humility and with a courteousness and kindness I hadn't seen before.

It is still difficult to put my finger on exactly what I experienced, but it wasn't the physical act of handing me a meal, but the way it was done – full of grace. That was the word that came to mind when I reflected on the experience later. Perhaps the best way of describing it is that it was the complete opposite of the service received in many restaurants in the UK, in which waiting staff sometimes bring with them a feeling of slight resentment or a level of superficiality. There was nothing at all like that at the meal in Buenos Aires, just people full of grace and love, serving food. The experience moved me so much, I had to leave the room and go out onto the balcony and cry.

Inevitably, there is much overlap between the different characteristics we are looking at day by day in these pages. It would be impossible to be full of grace or gracious in the true sense of these words without also showing humility, gentleness and love; but let's look have a deeper look now at this word 'grace', and what it is to be gracious. The word 'grace' is often used by religions to signify divine providence; for example, 'there but for the grace of God go I', which can be paraphrased as 'it could have equally well have been me that ended up in such an unfortunate situation, but for God's grace I am not'. Divine grace carries with it a sense of undeserving providence, so when we are acting graciously there are no expectations of rights or thanks from others for what we are doing; it is about giving of ourselves freely with no strings attached. Going back to the Argentinian experience, the servers didn't give the impression that they felt they were somehow lower than us because they were serving us; rather, I imagine they felt a sense of privilege and pride at being able to do so. Probably much more than that, they were delighted to be of service, with no chips on their shoulders whatsoever.

Perhaps the lack of grace in our Western society is because many of us are envious or jealous of the position, the money or power of others. It is impossible to exhibit grace if we are not content with who we are and our purpose in life. Many of us like to think that we are not at all influenced by the celebrity or fame that is endemic in our culture, but being completely disassociated from this is more difficult than we may imagine, with media surrounding us 24 hours a day. It is sometimes difficult not to wonder how a particular celebrity has managed to get to his or her position with so little talent; and we may even think, 'That should have been me.' Personally, I spent many years subconsciously wishing I was doing something else rather than giving my all to my current endeavours, which resulted in a lack of grace in many of my interactions with others at the time.

Even if you have no sense of an all-powerful being, it is helpful to reflect back to the definition of divine grace to help learn graciousness. In all religions that have the concept, there is a sense of undeserved merit. Those who act with grace towards others carry with them the sense that it is divine providence or luck, depending on your point of view, which enabled them to be in the position of leadership or responsibility that they find themselves in. In the Middle Ages, there were 'grace-and-favour houses', which provided free accommodation bestowed by a sovereign as an expression of gratitude to a subject (some still exist today). They carried with them the sense that the recipients didn't really deserve such a lavish gift, and they were an extravagance. Being gracious is about extravagantly giving to others.

I regularly listen to a business podcast where founders of well-known USA companies are interviewed for an hour by the presenter Guy Raz, who always finishes the interview with the same question: 'Do you consider that you have achieved success through luck or your own hard work?' I must have listened to at least 50 interviews and 9 out of 10 of these founders give a figure of 95 per cent or upwards of their success being attributable to luck, often describing this as being in the right place at the right time with the right idea. These very successful entrepreneurs feel a tremendous sense of grace or luck and know that their outcomes could have been so different with a few tiny changes in circumstances. Those who know their success stems not purely from their own endeavours are far more likely to be gracious in their dealings with others, and it is this kind of person, full of grace, who makes a great leader and often builds a very successful business.

Actions

So how can we be more gracious in our interactions with others today?

» In this moment, let's consciously remind ourselves that everything we have achieved isn't purely down to us. And at any point today when we are tempted to think that we are deserving of what we have, think again and consciously remember it is through grace (or luck).

» At least three times today verbally thank those around you for what they have done for you and then make that a daily habit.

» What act can you do today to be gracious? Could you give someone something they haven't earned or aren't expecting: an unexpected gift, the afternoon off, or perhaps you could unexpectedly take someone out for coffee or lunch?

DAY 6 » **Solitary**

Dictionary definition:

'The state of being... alone; seclusion.'
Dictionary.com

Quotes:

'It is a difficult lesson to learn today, to leave one's friends and family and deliberately practise the art of solitude for an hour or a day or a week. For me, the break is most difficult... And yet, once it is done, I find there is a quality to being alone that is incredibly precious. Life rushes back into the void, richer, more vivid, fuller than before!'
Anne Morrow Lindbergh, American author and aviator

'The truth is that solitude is the creative condition of genius, religious or secular, and the ultimate sterilising of it.'
Helen Waddell, Irish poet and playwright

'I live in that solitude which is painful in youth, but delicious in the years of maturity.'
Albert Einstein, German theoretical physicist

'If you are lonely when you're alone, you are in bad company.'
Jean-Paul Sartre, French philosopher

Insights

I remember reading Terry Waite's book *Taken on Trust* back in the nineties, in which he described the impact that more than four years in solitary confinement had on him. The book had a profound impact on me at the time, bringing me to tears, moved by the depth that someone can find within themselves when left alone with their thoughts. The idea of spending that amount of time alone is frightening for most of us and we have no idea whether we would get through it.

In an interview with the *Daily Telegraph* at the start of the coronavirus lockdown in 2020, Waite described how he was kept underground on a thin mattress and was only granted one visit to the bathroom each day. He was allowed no natural light or reading material and absolutely no contact with the outside world. He wasn't even allowed to see the guards: a blindfold was put over his eyes whenever a guard came into the room with his meal. So he didn't see another human being for years. In those extreme circumstances of being alone, Waite says he discovered things about himself that he was not especially proud of and says he had to learn to grow a greater acceptance of himself and work towards a deeper inner harmony.

And that last sentence is the key to the benefits of solitude and the reason we must choose some solitude as leaders. The adjective 'solitary' may be a strange one to describe someone who is a leader. Surely the whole point of being called a leader is that you are leading people and therefore you act as a figurehead for them. Yes, that is most certainly true for a good part of a leader's time, but great leaders will always ensure they spend some time in solitude. It is certainly no coincidence that many great leaders have spent long periods on their own, whether through their own choice or incarceration; for what happens in that quiet and sometimes lonely place forms the woman or man. These periods of solitude are not only places where we create new ideas and reflect on our activity, but also, probably more importantly, places that allow us to get to know our inner selves – something that all truly great leaders have achieved.

Even if we find it difficult, we must learn to be on our own, and embrace the solitude and learn to enjoy it. Now, there are introverts who just love to be on their own anyway and these people may need to discipline themselves to be on their own less; but when speaking to extroverts, I often recommend the huge benefits of carving out time to be alone. And it will be a discipline for you to ensure that this time is kept sacred. It may be hard at first, but I promise that you will start to look forward to it. In the personality tests I have done in the past, I come out as extrovert on some and introvert on others, so I imagine I am somewhere on the mid-line; but I absolutely know I need time on my own, and crave this time more if I have spent too many days with others on trips away from home.

I love the quote above from Anne Morrow Lindbergh, where she says, 'for me the break is the most difficult', which is about the discipline of breaking away from people and activities. When we spend time in solitude, this time can become incredibly precious to us and is like a daily meal that we miss if we haven't had it. We can all relate to the difficulty of pulling away from others with our busy – some would say over-busy – lives; it is in forcing ourselves to take the break where discipline is required. Lindbergh was a busy person, an author and aviator whose infant son was kidnapped for ransom and eventually killed; so she was no stranger to stress, busyness and hardship, yet she craved the time to be alone.

What is it we can do when alone that we can't do when we are surrounded by others? The answer lies in it being a period of self-examination. Time to reflect on what we are doing and our motivations for doing so. Time to examine whether some of what we do is out of hurt and pain, i.e. the conditioned self rather than the unconditioned self. Yes, there is a time to read and a time to listen to music or podcasts, but there is also a time to simply be on our own with nothing but ourselves for company. Our minds may wander and while there is nothing wrong with that, I have found the practice of meditation useful in helping me live in the present moment, enabling me to forget about the happenings of the previous 24 hours, and to quiet the mind from planning what I am going to do that day.

I am also fortunate enough to live in the countryside, so can easily escape my home office and be on my own with the birds and trees within minutes. This is something that many of us enjoyed for the first time during the initial coronavirus lockdown in 2020, and I have talked to many leaders who have now built this alone time into their schedules, and who now wonder how they ever functioned without it. Those who have experienced solitude and the benefits that it brings, will sometimes need to be 'selfish' in carving out that time away from others who may not understand, such as work colleagues or family members. And as long as it is not an excuse to get out of doing the washing-up or attending a meeting you really should be at, it is actually not selfish at all. Our solitary time energises us to be able to give more to others, those you serve in both business and family. Others will soon learn that ensuring we have that time alone will make us a better leader, parent, partner or friend.

Actions

What can we do today to learn to be alone?

» Take a walk on your own at lunchtime, or at another time today, and enjoy being on your own. Don't forget to turn your phone off!

» Why not schedule some alone time in your diary now for whenever you next have space when you can guarantee to be on your own for an hour with no agenda. Make this a regular occurrence even if you find it difficult.

» Make time to explain to your work colleagues and your loved ones the importance of your having some alone time each week – and encourage them to do the same.

DAY 7 » **Playful**

Dictionary definition:

'Full of fun and high spirits; frolicsome or sportive.'
Free Dictionary

Quotes:

'The very essence of playfulness is an openness to anything that may happen, the feeling that whatever happens, it's okay… you're either free to play, or you're not.'
John Cleese, English actor and comedian

'To me there is nothing more sacred than love and laughter, and there is nothing more prayerful than playfulness.'
Rajneesh, Indian mystic

'As God contains all good things, He must also contain a sense of playfulness – a gift he has shared with Creatures other than ourselves, as witness the tricks Crows play, and the sportiveness of Squirrels, and the frolicking of Kittens.'
Margaret Atwood, Canadian poet and novelist

'Many teachers think of children as immature adults. It might lead to better and more "respectful" teaching, if we thought of adults as atrophied children.'
Keith Johnstone, British-Canadian pioneer of improvisation theatre

Insights

Paul Lindley, founder of Ella's Kitchen, a successful baby and children's food brand, has written a beautiful book called *Little Wins: The Huge Power of Thinking Like a Toddler*. And there is no other area of life where children have more to teach adults than the area of playfulness or having fun. Lindley quotes James Brown, an American psychologist, who believes that the impact of play deprivation is significant in adults as well as children:

> Play-deprived adults are often rigid, humorless, inflexible and closed to trying out new options [...] Playfulness enhances the capacity to innovate, adapt and master changing circumstances. It is not just an escape. It can help us integrate and reconcile difficult or contradictory circumstances.

I was once a governor of a nursery school in a deprived area of London and, like all early-years education, the whole curriculum was based on learning through play. There was no actual teaching at all, just play and experimentation, and yet the school won awards across the capital for excellence in education. Many of us adults would benefit from the toddlers' example by learning through play. Often, we are far too serious and grown-up and need to learn to let our hair down and have fun. I love Keith Johnstone's thought that adults are atrophied children, rather than the way we often view them – as imperfect humans until they are adult.

At our company, Cotswold Fayre, we have five company values and by far the favourite of most of the team is: 'Have fun, get it done.' Even in the extremely busy and stressful times of year, I can often hear peals of laughter ringing out around the office, and I'm sure customers calling on the phone can hear it too – although if they are ringing to complain about something, perhaps this may be one of the few times they don't want to hear joviality!

In fact, I did once have a complaint from a rather serious customer about us having too much fun. We used to regularly work with a Magic Circle magician at our trade shows. The thinking was that if we could have some fun while we were pushing for new business, it would portray the right kind of image and attract the right customers. They would remember us better than the various other wholesalers around us, some of who, without being rude, were various shades of grey. Simon the magician would do close-up magic with customers and potential customers as they stopped by our stand. One customer (from Yorkshire

– a complete coincidence I am sure) stopped in his tracks and was so angry he almost had steam coming out of his ears. He asked me why we were wasting money on a magician when we could have been giving him better prices, and then stomped off down the aisle.

I don't think it is a coincidence that, in an anonymous survey amongst our team a few years ago, when we asked the question, 'Do you enjoy coming to work?' we had 100 per cent 'yeses' as answers. It is because our people have fun at work. Yes, we do have serious issues and problems like any other company, but learning to play is foundational to being successful and productive. In fact, on some days at Paul Lindley's Ella's Kitchen office, you might think you had walked into a children's play area rather than one of the most successful fast-moving consumer goods (FMCG) brands from the past 20 years. A few years ago, they even turned one of their meeting rooms into a ball pit! That this level of fun continues long after Paul sold the company shows how well this value is embedded in their culture.

Being playful is essential for creativity. In fact, many tech companies build in time for employees to play around and do their own thing completely away from any company agenda, enabling some remarkable creativity to occur. The now famous example of this is at 3M, who for a long time had a philosophy of allowing time for their employees to play. One day, one of their teams was experimenting and trying to develop a very strong glue, which failed miserably and was probably the world's weakest glue; but it had enough stickiness to become the company's most successful product: Post-it Notes. Create a workplace with too much professionalism and seriousness and it will not be a company that adapts creatively to new situations – something that is more necessary now than at any other point in history, as the world changes at an ever-increasing rate.

We have all had the experience of trying to remember someone's name, for example, and we can't remember it despite straining every neurone; then, later that day, when you are wandering around not thinking of anything, the name will pop into your mind. Play is a little like that: the best ideas and creativity come when the creative part of the brain is engaged in play. It helps enormously that we are actively moving away from the intellectual, cerebral part of our brain and into another space. At the start of many of our meetings at Cotswold Fayre, we do an activity that is playful or humorous – and I guarantee that you too will have better, more productive meetings if you institute something like this, if you don't already. Don't be tempted to think in a meeting that you are wasting time by doing something seemingly trivial, which is eating into time required for the 'business part'. Making part of the meeting playful will speed up the decision-making part of the meeting as the creative and intuitive parts of people's brains will be more engaged.

The same is true in the world of professional speaking, in which I am a relative newcomer. I am sure those talks you can remember having the largest impact on you are the ones where there was an element of humour or playfulness. Nowhere is this clearer than in school assemblies. I remember the murmur of excitement that went around the assembly hall when we could see that the teacher giving the talk that morning was the one who always made us laugh yet had a serious point to make. Conversely, I remember the groans when the day's speaker was the teacher who just delivered the words with no sense of fun. People will remember what we say when we have engaged their emotions; so let's be playful if we desire lasting change, not just when on the stage but in our everyday leadership activities.

Actions

Today, let's learn to play:

» Do other people consider you to be playful or serious? What could you do to bring more fun to your leadership?

» Think now of a few playful habits you could bring in to make your workplace more fun. If you do this as a leader, it will give other people permission to follow your example in their own meetings.

» If you run regular meetings, then think of a playful exercise you can start to do at the start of your next meeting to engage the creative right-half of people's brains. For example, on a Zoom call recently, the early arrivals all grabbed a hat and wore it so those arriving late to the meeting wondered what on earth was going on!

DAY 8 » **Servant-like**

Dictionary definition:

> 'One who expresses submission, recognizance, or debt to another.'
> *Free Dictionary*

Quotes:

> 'The servant-leader is servant first... It begins with the natural feeling that one wants to serve, to serve first. Then conscious choice brings one to aspire to lead. That person is sharply different from one who is leader first.'
> *Robert K. Greenleaf, American founder of Modern Servant-Leadership movement*

> 'Servant-leadership is more than a concept, it is a fact. Any great leader, by which I also mean an ethical leader of any group, will see herself or himself as a servant of that group and will act accordingly.'
> *M. Scott Peck, American psychiatrist*

> 'Service is the rent that you pay for room on this earth.'
> *Shirley Chisholm, first Black woman elected to USA Congress*

> 'Everybody can be great... because anybody can serve. You don't have to have a college degree to serve.'
> *Martin Luther King, Jr., American civil rights activist*

Insights

Ask someone of a certain age to think of someone who demonstrated how to be a servant-leader and many of us will think of the same person: an Albanian nun who worked for decades in the slums of Kolkata, India – Mother Teresa. A civil servant who worked with her for more than a decade described her in the *Straits Times*, Singapore as being 'the embodiment of a servant leader'. As in the Robert K. Greenleaf quote, she was a servant first, rather than a leader first. How different to many leaders, who are driven by the desire for power or material possessions. This observer of Mother Teresa described those who take either a leader-first or servant-first approach as representing two extreme types of person, between which there are various shades and blends of human nature. Mother Teresa saw herself as being a servant first, out of which her leadership arose. For her, leading was a form of service, which is how it is meant to be – yet very different from some of the leadership we see today in the West. The writer finishes by describing the true test of servant-leadership as being the 'positive growth of the people she or he leads'.

Yet how often do we see this kind of leadership within businesses, organisations or even religious institutions today? Many leaders expect to be served, rather than serve. In the corporate world, they expect salaries sometimes more than 200 to 300 times the average wage in their company, so large they can afford to employ servants in their homes in some cases. They would never expect to have to make their own tea or coffee, let alone make one for others in their office. How have we come so far away from leadership as a position of servanthood? It is considered strange to be a servant-leader in some quarters. In our reception area at our offices, there is a 'rogue's gallery' of photos of all the people in the company, which are arranged in frames in a random order. Several visitors have mentioned that it is odd that I and the other leaders aren't positioned at the top, to show the hierarchy. That would be odd to me; if anything, the leaders should be at the bottom, to illustrate their support of those above them.

Those with some knowledge of the Bible will be very familiar with the story of Jesus washing his disciples' feet. He was doing the work of a servant, or even a slave, for a bunch of men who had been in complete awe of him as their leader for the past three years; and in this way he demonstrated true leadership. How completely upside down, yet wonderful that a leader didn't consider himself above the people that he was leading. Simon Sinek's excellent book *Leaders Eat Last* explores the whole concept of servant-leadership and takes its title from the American Marine Corps, where the practice is that leaders are always served last at mealtimes. It is part of their culture for these marine leaders to eat last, because they know that leadership is about putting those you are leading first.

Much of our personal experience of our leaders has been the opposite, and like it or not, this can be subconsciously passed on to us, so when we find ourselves in a position of leadership we behave in the ways that others have modelled to us. Leaders with high public profiles – politicians, corporate CEOs and the like – are also demonstrating the wrong kind of leadership in many cases, so our children grow up thinking this is what leadership looks like. Even worse, many of us have been badly hurt by leaders not exhibiting servant qualities and still carry the scars from them. We have all known leaders who have had a superior air around them, lauded it over us, bullied us or, even worse, abused us. This form of leadership comes from the conditioned self and has no place in today's world. True leadership is about metaphorically wrapping a towel around your waist and cleaning all the dirt and grime off your followers' feet and enjoying serving others. Many leaders, commonly men, have carried a whip rather than a towel.

In December 2018, I went on a spiritual walk in India with a modern mystic and 12 fellow leaders from a mix of cultural backgrounds. We walked around 10 to 15 miles daily, missed lunch every day and slept on temple floors at night time. None of us had ever done anything like this before. For eight days, our leader demonstrated servant-leadership in a way seldom seen and this form of leadership became contagious throughout the group. One evening, after a 10-hour walk, while I was resting on my bed (a sleeping bag on the floor), an Indian member of the group offered to massage my feet. To be honest, I was uncomfortable with this, as earlier that day I had apologised on behalf of my British ancestors for the atrocities wrought in colonial India. The act of servanthood should really have been the other way around, but he wasn't going to let me win that argument. For 30 minutes or so, I experienced true servanthood from another leader and had a glimpse of real leadership in that moment: someone who would take the lowest place and put others first. It can be a spiritual experience but one we must carry into our lives in a practical way, so that those who follow us really know that we are putting them first.

Perhaps a change in heart and attitude is necessary first as it is easy to slip into a mode of authority without the desire to serve those who follow us. We desperately need more examples of servant-leadership and far less of the command-and-control leadership we have come to know all too well – the masculine, egoistical type, which is diametrically opposite to what I am describing here. Many more examples of servant-like behaviour are being exhibited in the 21st century, but we must hasten the journey towards servant-leadership becoming the norm, and that, of course, starts with us.

Actions

So, how can we be a servant today?

» Reflect for a few minutes on how you could serve others more as a leader. Could it be in what you say, how you write to people on email, how you do and say things? Do you really serve or do you expect other people to serve you?

» Perhaps think of a task that you don't normally do at home or work and surprise others by being a servant and carrying it out today.

» If we are a leader, we sometimes expect things to happen for us that wouldn't happen for others, such as the largest desk or the centre seat at a board meeting. Perhaps find a way of taking the lowest place in a physical way today. Mix it up.

DAY 9 » **Thankful**

Dictionary definition:

'Conscious of benefit received.'
Merriam-Webster Dictionary

Quotes:

'Let us rise up and be thankful, for if we didn't learn a lot today, at least we learned a little, and if we didn't learn a little, at least we didn't get sick, and if we got sick, at least we didn't die; so, let us all be thankful.'
Buddha, Indian philosopher and spiritual teacher

'It's impossible to feel sad or have any negative feeling when you're grateful. If you're in the midst of a difficult situation, look for something to be grateful for.'
Rhonda Byrne, Australian TV writer and producer

'If the only prayer you ever say in your entire life is thank you, it will be enough.'
Meister Eckhart, German theologian, philosopher and mystic

'Be thankful for what you have; you'll end up having more. If you concentrate on what you don't have, you will never, ever have enough.'
Oprah Winfrey, American chat show host

Insights

There is one practice that has the power to change our lives in a remarkable way and it is the practice of thankfulness. Making a conscious effort to be thankful daily will help build into our lives many of the other characteristics we desire. Being thankful on a regular basis can bring joy, humility, generosity and even resilience into our lives. It is easy to live in a spirit of thankfulness on our good days; mere amateurs can do that! What is more difficult is the practice of being thankful when stuff is going down and we are battling against adversity, whether personal or business related.

Being thankful is transformative and we will all enjoy better mental health with increased gratitude. Some cultures are by nature more thankful than others. Living in the UK, I am sadly aware that we are not one of those, with many of us being predisposed to negativity rather than positivity. Whether there is a correlation between the weather and thankfulness I am not sure, but British people often start a conversation by moaning about the weather and all too often their mood seems to be influenced by it too. It is a good practice to learn to be thankful on the rainy and cold days as well as the sunny ones, both literally and metaphorically.

The link between thankfulness and happiness is not just anecdotal but scientifically proven. Dr Robert A. Emmons, a professor at the University of California, demonstrates this in his book *Thanks!* By researching different groups of people and control groups, he shows through various experiments that people can increase their 'set-point' for happiness by as much as 25 per cent. Dr Emmons recommends keeping a gratitude journal and shows that those who do this report sleeping better and having more energy even after just three weeks. Clearly there is a link between thankfulness and good physical health, as well as the more obvious mental health benefits.

I read Emmons's excellent book in the early summer of 2019 and was challenged to bring more thankfulness into my life. Since then I have made it a habit to pause to give thanks at different points during the day. Later that summer, our wholesale business made a significant change to its logistics model with the main aim of reducing our carbon impact in distribution by a massive 46 per cent. Due to a combination of factors outside our control, the warehouse move went wrong and for many weeks customers were receiving terrible service from us and there was a great deal of pressure on the whole management team, particularly me as their leader. It is not a great thing – to dread going into work as the CEO. During this time, I put into practice a discipline of thankfulness and in my slot allocated for quiet at the start of each day, I declared out loud that I was actively thankful for three things. There is so much to be thankful for, even when it seems everything is going pear-shaped. Being thankful helps put the bad events into the proper perspective compared to the important things in life such as family, health and having food on the table, the latter of which takes us out of the bottom 10 per cent of the world's population.

Reflecting on that summer, it was very similar to a previous time in the company's history in 2014, which almost took the company and me personally to complete meltdown. I wasn't actively practising thankfulness in 2014, which made the personal toll on my own mental health far more serious. Back to 2019 – and we came through the despair and frustration after about three months. The word used by the team to describe how we as a company had developed during that time was 'resilience'. I am convinced a significant part of that resilience came from the practice of thankfulness that we introduced into company meetings.

Towards the end of that traumatic three months, I heard of two events that helped me realise why we can and must always be thankful. I was told in a phone call from my sister about a school friend who had had an accident on holiday and ended up as a paraplegic. Then, within a week of that, I heard that the warehouse of another wholesaler had been burned down in an arson attack. Any troubles our company had endured paled into complete insignificance.

Whether you keep a gratitude journal or simply remember to be thankful for three or four things at the beginning and/or end of each day, I promise you will notice the difference. Even if you do not believe in a power outside ourselves to whom to offer thanks, it is possible just to sit in an attitude of thankfulness while mentioning the items you are grateful for.

There are many, many people in this world who have far less to be thankful for than we do. If you are reading this book, then you are probably in the top 5 per cent of global affluence and I thoroughly recommend spending time working alongside those in poorer situations than you, either in your own country or in another global community. We can surely learn much from them, both by realising how privileged we are and how thankful those that have so little are for what they do have.

Finally, as well as having a thankful attitude of heart, let's grow in our appreciation of others when they do anything for us. Rather than murmuring thanks under our breath, really thank them: look into their eyes and show them true gratitude, like you mean it. Even for those people who are paid to carry out tasks for you, it doesn't mean that you don't give thanks when they do it. Real gratitude and appreciation will do them good, as well as you. Taking things for granted is a Western disease and being a thankful leader will help cure us from this ill as well as improving the physical and mental health of ourselves and those who work with us.

Actions

Today, let's actively be thankful:

» Write down or say out loud now three things to be thankful for. They may be physical possessions, relationships or gratitude for circumstances from your past. Do this each day for a week, and hopefully by then it will become a habit.

» At any times of stress during today, stop what you are doing, step out of the room, or go for a short walk, and practise being thankful for what you have.

» Actively thank others today when they bring you something, such as a cup of tea or coffee. Look into their eyes and verbalise your thanks more than usual with a smile. You will brighten up both your days.

DAY 10 » **Kind**

Dictionary definition:

'Of a sympathetic or helpful nature.'
  Merriam-Webster Dictionary

Quotes:

'How lovely to think that no one need wait a moment, we can start now, start slowly changing the world! How lovely that everyone, great and small, can make their contribution toward introducing justice straightaway... And you can always, always give something, even if it is only kindness!'
  Anne Frank, German-Dutch diarist of Jewish origin

'As the rain falls on the just and unjust alike, let your heart be untroubled by judgments and let your kindness rain down on all.'
  Buddha, Indian philosopher and spiritual teacher

'No kind action ever stops with itself. One kind action leads to another. Good example is followed. A single act of kindness throws out roots in all directions, and the roots spring up and make new trees. The greatest work that kindness does to others is that it makes them kind themselves.'
  Amelia Earhart, American aviator and poet

'Kindness in words creates confidence. Kindness in thinking creates profoundness. Kindness in giving creates love.'
  Lao Tzu, ancient Chinese philosopher

Insights

One of the main themes to emerge out of the *Independent* newspaper report on the horrific bombings at the Ariana Grande concert in Manchester in 2017 was 'kindness'. Reporters described how ordinary people reacted with kindness and bravery when helping those in need. If you remember, these acts of kindness took place initially in the absence of the Fire and Rescue Service, who were kept away from the scene by their leaders in the immediate aftermath of the disaster. Local residents offered the afflicted concert goers and their parents places to stay, and taxi drivers offered free rides to those involved across the city. The spirit of kindness of the people of Manchester was an amazing display of resilience in the face of tragedy. The prime minister at the time, Theresa May, said: 'While we experienced the worst of humanity in Manchester last night, we also saw the best. The attempt to divide us met countless acts of kindness that brought people closer together and, in the days ahead, those must be the things that we remember.'

The word 'kindness' was much used in many other reports of the incident in connection with how Mancunians reacted. Now, growing up in that great city, I know it to be a particularly kind and friendly place, but I am sure that kindness would have been demonstrated in any city in such adversity. I believe that most human beings are naturally kind and this comes to the fore in difficult circumstances. What we may need to work harder at is letting out our kindness in everyday circumstances.

What exactly is 'kindness' and how is it different to being 'good' or 'compassionate' or various other characteristics that we will also be looking at? The word 'kindness' certainly implies an act, no matter how small, of helping someone. Like 'compassion', it is very much an active word but implicit in its definition is the everyday nature of being kind; whereas the word 'compassion' is normally used of a particular situation that has stirred the emotions. If we are kind, then we will regularly demonstrate kindness to others as it is inherent in our nature. That's why for many people, our natural instincts of kindness result in some amazing actions in a crisis or emergency.

Various organisations and charities have been set up around the world to promote random acts of kindness – and with one very good reason. Kindness is good for us and good for the world. It has been scientifically proven that those who perform acts of kindness on a regular basis enjoy better health and live longer than those who are less kind. That's because neurochemicals such as serotonin, oxytocin and endorphins are released into our bloodstream when we perform an act of kindness. Not only that, but kindness eases anxiety, it is good for our heart and mental health, and can prevent illness. Those who practise acts of kindness will be aware of this; there is a bounce in your step and a smile inside when you have performed an act of kindness.

So if we are being kind to ourselves when we are kind to others, so why don't we all live in a kinder world? The answer often lies in our conditioned behaviour. Perhaps we were hurt in some way when being kind to others as a child, which caused us to retreat from being kind as an adult so as to avoid the risk of more hurt. It is all too easy to go inside ourselves when we are feeling down and depressed. Instead, it is often by doing precisely what we might not feel like doing – by stepping outside ourselves at these challenging times – that we might start to feel better. Using the cerebral part of our brains to set an intention to be kind, then performing an act of kindness will release chemicals in our brains and give rise to emotions that will make us feel better. How easy is that? It is simply down to our positive choice in the first place.

Another interesting fact about kindness is that it is contagious. To use a trivial example, we will all have been in two different types of traffic jams: those where every driver refuses to give an inch and guards their space in the queue ferociously, and others where one driver shows kindness and lets in several other cars. This behaviour then spreads to other drivers, who also start letting people in, and the kindness spreads. In a study by Jamil Zaki in July 2016 called 'Kindness Contagion', he concluded: 'that people do not only imitate the particulars of positive actions but also the spirit underlying them. This implies that kindness itself is contagious, and that it can cascade across people, taking on new forms along the way.' The power of kindness, if you reflect on it, is enormous and can potentially change communities, cities, nations and even the world. To a small degree, this was one very positive effect of the coronavirus pandemic in 2020; acts of kindness seemed to follow the virus around the globe and replicated almost as fast. This gives me hope for an ongoing kindness pandemic, which could transform the world for good.

Being kind also means being aware of the world around us. In his book *21 Lessons for the 21st Century*, Yuval Noah Harari describes what he calls one of the nastiest experiments in the history of social sciences: in 1970, some trainee ministers in the Presbyterian Church were asked to hurry to a distant lecture hall and give a talk on the parable of the Good Samaritan. (The irony was intentional because in this well-known story, a man is beaten and robbed and left for dead on the roadside. Two religious people walk on by, whereas the guy who helps him is from a different ethnic group that should have made him his enemy.) Now, those organising this experiment had put a shabbily dressed person in a doorway along the student ministers' route, who called out for help as they rushed past. The trainee ministers were put into groups which had varying degrees of time pressure placed on them. In the group that had the most pressure put on them, most of the trainee ministers did not stop to ask whether the beggar was OK, let alone help him. They were so focused on the task in hand that they couldn't see the real needs in the world around them. Are we like this as leaders, too busy and pressurised most of the time to be kind?

Let's try to keep looking out for others even when we are busy and find opportunities to show kindness. That way, it will become a habit and we may be called kind by others. As one of the American kindness charities puts it in their strapline, let's 'make kindness the norm'.

Actions

Let's make today a day for random acts of kindness:

» First, though, let's reflect on why we have not been kind or where we have been so caught up in our own little world, we have not been kind to others. If any particular incidents come to mind, imagine the person you have been unkind to and say sorry to them out loud, as if they were in the room.

» Now plan an act of kindness to do today to someone who has not necessarily always been kind to you. Write it down in your journal.

» Finally, look for other opportunities today to be randomly kind to a stranger. It could be something small (such as leaving enough money for a coffee for the next person to come into the coffee shop) or something quite extraordinary. Spontaneity is the key.

DAY 11 » **Generous**

Dictionary definition:

'Willing and liberal in giving away one's money, time etc.: munificent.'
Collins English Dictionary

Quotes:

'The most generous persons are those who give silently without hope of praise or reward.'
Carol Ryrie Brink, American author

'We make a living by what we get, but we make a life by what we give.'
Winston Churchill, former British prime minister

'Generosity is giving more than you can, and pride is taking less than you need.'
Khalil Gibran, Lebanese philosopher, writer, poet and artist

'Generosity with strings is not generosity: it is a deal.'
Marya Mannes, American author and critic

Insights

There's an old story about a man from the country who knocked on a monastery door. When the monk at the gatehouse opened up, he gave the monk a huge bunch of grapes, the finest from his vineyard. The monk told the man that he would take them to the abbot immediately, but the vineyard owner told the monk that the grapes were actually for him, not the abbot, as he had been very kind to him. Once, when the man's crop had been destroyed by drought, the monk had given him bread and wine every day. The monk took the grapes and spent the entire morning admiring them without eating any. Later in the day, he decided anyway to deliver the gift to the abbot, who had always encouraged him with words of wisdom.

The abbot was very pleased with the grapes, but he recalled that there was a sick brother in the monastery and thought he should have the grapes instead to cheer him up. But the sick brother decided that the monastery's cook was more deserving of the grapes, as he had looked after the sick monk for a long time. The cook was amazed at the beauty of the grapes. So perfect were they that no one would appreciate them more than the sexton; many at the monastery considered him a holy man and he would be best qualified to value this marvel of nature. The sexton, in turn, gave the grapes as a gift to the youngest novice, that he might understand that the work of God is found in the smallest details of creation. When the novice received them, he remembered the first time he came to the monastery, and the person who had opened the gates for him; it was that gesture which allowed him to be among this community of people, who knew how to value the wonders of life. So, just before nightfall, the novice took the grapes to the monk at the gate, who now truly understood that the grapes were destined for him, so ate them and fell into a deep sleep. The circle of generosity was closed.

The simple message from this story is one we have all heard many times over: 'give and it will be given back to you' or 'what goes around comes around'. There are stories within most cultures that encourage us to be generous, because those who give generously will receive back more abundantly. Yet how much do we believe this? The evidence of today's Western culture suggests many don't. The challenge for all of us is that it is sometimes difficult for us to let go and trust enough to give to others with no strings attached. Too much of our generosity is transactional or contractual, which is not true generosity; nor is it 'giving more than we can', as defined in today's quote from Kahlil Gibran.

The Hindu tradition talks of abundance, which is the ultimate place of living with no thought or worry about how giving to others might result in leaving ourselves short. In fact, this tradition would say that those who worry about self-preservation, and never give beyond their means, will not enjoy the fruits of generosity. Many of us will have met very wealthy people, who despite having more money and possessions than most, seem to worry more about losing what they have than those with much less. Sometimes, this anxiety stems from poverty in childhood; for example, when a parent has squandered money, leaving the family short. It is difficult, though not impossible, to break this cycle. Those whose worries stop them from giving to others may need help to enable them to experience the true happiness that flows from being extremely generous.

The great sadness is that so many in our Western culture are trapped in unhappiness because they haven't experienced the joy of giving freely. I remember once being given some money by a very generous person to buy as many turkeys as I could to give to impoverished families in London on Christmas Eve. It was a privilege to be able to enjoy the fruits of that generosity, which wasn't even my own, and it brought tears to my eyes to see the pleasure that it gave to the recipients. In Matthew's version of Jesus' Sermon on the Mount, he says it is more blessed to give than receive. The word 'blessed' literally translates as 'happy', so we could paraphrase the sentence: 'If you want to be happy, give to others.' In our heart of hearts, we all know this is true. When we were children, we greatly enjoyed receiving presents, but as we become older, true joy is in the giving, not the receiving, of gifts.

How do we carry this generosity into the workplace as a leader? Primarily, if we have the authority, it is by being over-the-top in our generosity to our teams and employees. Generosity is not about an internal calculation of working out how we will get the money or time back. Neither is it about whether they deserve it, true generosity is about giving generously in pay, bonuses and holidays. As we understand abundance and generosity, we know we will always receive back when we are generous, and nowhere is this truer than in the workplace. Remember the monks in the story earlier: generosity, like kindness, is contagious, and most human beings will behave generously if they are shown generosity. Occasionally, people may take advantage of our generosity, but this does not mean the principle is wrong; it just means that the circle of generosity is broken temporarily. Reverting to miserliness is certainly not the answer. However, trust issues will need to be discussed if we are taken advantage of, so generosity can once more flow.

Many magnanimous souls would much rather leave a legacy in other people's lives by their generosity while they are alive than leave a large stash of cash to others when they die. I recently went to the funeral of a generous man, one of our company's suppliers. The building was packed, and everyone was given the opportunity to tell tales of his generosity. It was an incredible event, and the impact this man had on others through his decades of generosity was profound. If more leaders lived their lives like him, we would have a very different world. As Winston Churchill wisely said, 'We make a life by what we give'.

Actions

Let's be generous today:

» Reflect upon whether you are experiencing the joy of being generous. Recall a time when you were generous and remember those good feelings. Now, don't you want to enjoy that more? How can you create those feelings more often through your generosity?

» Consider whether you have a fear of being without money or possessions. Do you hold on to possessions and money where you could release others by your generosity?

» At work or home today, think of an act of an anonymous act of generosity you could do – and then do it!

DAY 12 » **Creative**

Dictionary definition:

'Characterized by originality of thought; having or showing imagination.'
Collins English Dictionary

Quotes:

'Every child is an artist. The problem is how to remain an artist once he grows up.'
Pablo Picasso, Spanish artist

'Creativity is just connecting things. When you ask creative people how they did something, they feel a little guilty because they didn't really do it, they just saw something. It seemed obvious to them after a while.'
Steve Jobs, American entrepreneur

'The most regretful people on earth are those who felt the call to creative work, who felt their own creative power restive and uprising, and gave to it neither power nor time.'
Mary Oliver, American poet

'You see things; and you say, "Why?" But I dream things that never were; and I say, "Why not?"'
George Bernard Shaw, Irish playwright

Insights

One of my great desires in life as a leader is to see people expressing their creativity; and one of my greatest sadnesses is when creativity is hidden, repressed or even squashed completely. The education system in the UK is great in some ways, but also responsible for much of the repression of creativity in this country. Having a syllabus that rewards only academic results means our creative side is considered low priority, and often not given the time it deserves. Our education only educates one half of the brain, the logical left-hand side, and it virtually ignores the right-hand side, the creative part. I am fortunate to be a naturally creative person but went to a school where science was encouraged more than the arts and creativity, so, like many of my peers, ended up going down the 'wrong' route for my ability. I have since managed to redeem some of those 'lost' years, but it has probably taken a decent part of my adult life to do so.

I love the Picasso quote about every child being an artist, the problem being staying an artist as we grow up. So, let's discuss what stifles our creativity before going on to look at some tips for regaining it. The first inhibitor is the self-consciousness that many of us develop as teenagers and never quite shake off for the rest of our lives. Some would say this impacts girls more than boys, but I think it has an equal and massive impact on all of us. You only have to look at the difference between young children and many teenagers to see what I mean. Teenagers are not given enough affirmation about their abilities or their bodies, and carry that self-consciousness right through to adulthood, which inhibits the freedom to express themselves, and their creativity often dies.

Second, and closely connected to the first inhibitor, is the fear of what others think, i.e. the fear of failure. It is important to create for your own enjoyment first and foremost, and having the attitude 'who cares what others think' is a great mentality. As I write these words in my garden, I have no idea whether these words will ever be published, and I don't care – I am enjoying the process of learning and creating, which is enough for me in this moment. Maybe my own children or grandchildren will read these pages, and it is worth writing for them, because I believe in this stuff and think it will help them. Another part of that fear relates to wanting a creation to be perfect first time round, although it rarely will be, as good creations take time. Leonardo da Vinci is understood to have worked on the *Mona Lisa* for 14 years, and I am sure there were plenty of rubbings-out along the way.

We live in a culture where failure is not rewarded; in fact, the opposite is true, we are often criticised for failure, yet without a degree of failure there is very little creativity. We would do well to create a culture in our workplaces where failure is not looked down on. As individuals, we need to learn to ignore the fear of failure and to be prepared to look like fools to others, something I do regularly. In George Bernard Shaw's words, many of the 'whys' or reasons for not creating come from people's fears. In his now famous Ted Talk, Astro Teller talks about his work as head of X (formerly Google X) in creating a culture where failure is celebrated and even rewarded with bonuses. I love this. It was also encouraging to note that when recently gathering data for a Research and Development tax rebate claim for some of our company's innovations, we were told that having a degree of failure in the project counted positively towards our claim. The message being: failure means they are pushing the boundaries.

Third, as leaders, apart from creating a positive culture where failure is not penalised but celebrated, there must also be encouragement for people to be themselves at work. Too many of us have for years behaved at work how other people have wanted us to behave, or rather how we think others have wanted us to behave, rather than simply being ourselves. The younger generations are helping us in this area, as they are generally freer to be themselves without hiding behind metaphorical masks. Encouraging this atmosphere in your business will release more creativity for everyone in the organisation, maybe even you too!

So, after putting in place some of these ideas to increase creativity in ourselves and our workplaces, what can we do on a practical level to stimulate our own creative juices? Exercise often helps us, such as going to the gym or going for a run or brisk walk, just to stay in good physical condition. Also relaxing and chilling out can help too. It's an old cliché, but that moment of finding inspiration in the bath contains some truth. If you are struggling for inspiration, it may sometimes help to be creative in a completely different medium in order to start flowing, and then move back to the original area of creativity. For example, I was hoping to write this morning, but knew I wasn't in the right frame of mind, so I pottered around the garden for a while and planted some bedding plants, felt more inspired and came back to writing this afternoon. The creative activity in the garden helped trigger the creative right-hand side of my brain.

Another interesting fact that may help here is to know that science has shown that the creative right-hand side of our brain is very active at night-time. I have woken up on several mornings with something creative burning, which I've needed to write down as soon as possible.

Sometimes that difficult email and an idea for a new vlog are there in my mind after waking and I just need to download them onto a keyboard. There are people who set their creative brain homework while they are asleep by journaling about the areas they are struggling to find creative solutions to before they go to sleep, and then letting the subconscious brain work on them while they are sleeping.

Ernest Hemingway seems to have lived by this principle: 'I had learned already never to empty the well of my writing, but always to stop when there was still something there in the deep part of the well, and let it refill at night from the springs that fed it.' And I would certainly recommend keeping a notebook to hand for both before and after sleep, to make the most of our nighttime creativity.

Actions

Let's allow our creativity to flow today:

» To what extent have you have masked or repressed your creativity? Think about how you could stimulate more creativity, whether at work or home, and journal any ideas that come to mind.

» Think about how failure is viewed in your workplace. Is it condemned or celebrated? Has your workplace culture inhibited creativity? What could change?

» Tonight, give your subconscious mind some night-time homework. Before you go to sleep, write down in your journal some areas where you need creative inspiration and see what happens when you wake up. Be prepared to be surprised!

DAY 13 » **Content**

Dictionary definition:

'Feeling or showing satisfaction with one's possessions, status, or situation.'
Merriam-Webster Dictionary

Quotes:

'I am not saying this because I am in need, for I have learned to be content whatever the circumstances.'
Paul the Apostle

'Content makes poor men rich; discontent makes rich men poor.'
Benjamin Franklin, British-American polymath

'Be thankful for what you have; you'll end up having more. If you concentrate on what you don't have, you will never, ever have enough.'
Oprah Winfrey, American chat show host

'Happiness consists not in having much, but in being content with little.'
Marguerite Gardiner, Irish novelist and journalist

Insights

In *The Future We Choose*, Christiana Figueres and Tom Rivett-Carnac remind us of a story first made popular by Paulo Coelho – of a content fisherman, relaxing on the beach near his little village after catching a few big fish. A businessman, no doubt on holiday, wanders past, notices the fish and asks the fisherman how long it took to catch them. When finding out it didn't take very long, the visitor asks the fisherman why he doesn't spend more time at sea and catch more fish. The fisherman replies that the fish are plenty to feed his family and after fishing in the early morning, he can play with his kids, have an afternoon nap with his wife and then join his friends for drinks and music-making in the evening.

The businessman suggests that he could loan money to the fisherman in order to make him more successful. This way he could spend more time at sea, buy a larger boat to catch more fish and make more money. He could then invest in more boats and set up a large fishing company. Over time, the company could be listed on the stock exchange and make the fisherman millions. 'Then what?' asks the fisherman. The businessman proudly explains that then the fisherman can retire. He can finally catch a few fish in the early morning and after fishing, he can play with his kids, have an afternoon nap with his wife and then join his friends for drinks and music-making in the evening.

It is an old story yet still makes the point very well. The drive for higher growth and the constant need for more are often what leave us discontented. The fisherman in the story was content with what he had and didn't need a Western businessman to tell him how to run his life. In fact, this is another lesson that those in the developing world can teach those living in more industrialised nations. Simplicity of life is not the bad thing that our Western education and upbringing have conditioned us to think that it is. In business, for example, the never-ending drive for growth and profit can create a discontentment that impacts our own wellbeing.

Essential to being content is being able to grasp the concept of 'enough'. Many of us in the West are not content because we don't think we have enough, when we have had plenty for years and simply haven't learned to appreciate it. If the industrialised world grasped this concept a little more strongly, the planet would not be in the state it is in today. This leads me on to a paradox, though, for those of us who see how much needs to change in the world in order to reverse climate change or reduce global poverty. How do we reconcile our ambition or purpose to make the world a better place with a contentment with where we are today? Can we be content if we are unhappy with the injustice in the world or the state of the planet, and desperate to see change? I believe we must try to reconcile those two seeming opposites. This can be a tough dilemma if, like me, you are driven to disrupt the status quo. However, there must be a place we can reach where we are content with who we are and what we are doing, but also be desirous of change. Reconciling the dichotomy relates to discovering our purpose and being crystal clear about the part we are called to play. We cannot change the world overnight and being content to play our part, whether large or small, while letting others play their part too, is surely part of the answer.

In terms of material possessions, many of us could learn to be content with much less. This is often one of the main discoveries for the teams I take to Western Kenya: the ability of those with very little to be completely content, and to be delighted with small things. Seeing the joy on teenagers' faces when we give them items from the UK that our own teenagers wouldn't even notice is humbling and changes us on the inside. I would encourage everyone to immerse themselves for a week or two in an impoverished community in the world in order to gain a different perspective and learn what it is to have enough. Only this morning, I overheard a conversation between two people, one of whom had just moved to a new house, saying that they had already moved two large lorry loads of possessions and only had two more lorry loads to move. Do we really need all that stuff?

Much has been written about the Danish word *hygge* meaning a sense of cosiness, comfort and contentment, but I would like here to introduce another Scandinavian concept, this time from Sweden: *lagom*. The word is an Old Norse form of the word 'law' and it also means 'the right amount' in Swedish. The word originates from the Vikings, who, when gathered around a fire in the evening, would pass around horns full of mead. Everyone was expected to sip their fair share, leaving enough for others. Enough. This reminds us of the story of Goldilocks, in which each member of the bear family had enough. If only we all used the principle of *lagom* in terms of the world's resources.

I count it a privilege to have experienced a few times in my early adult life when I had very little and, on a few occasions, when I didn't know where the money was coming from to pay the mortgage at the end of the month. In more recent times, I have been blessed with having more. However, a key to contentment is to be happy in either situation. Refusing to allow our financial fluidity to impact our identity as people is important – and a lesson I am still learning. Being thankful for what we do have is incredibly important too, so perhaps also go back and look at those actions too as well as those that follow here.

Actions

Let's actively decide to be more content today:

» Reflect for a moment on how content you are with what you are doing, where you are living, who you are living with. Very rarely is the grass truly greener on the other side... Are you always living for tomorrow rather than enjoying today? Stop now for a few moments and be content with today.

» Are you someone who suffers from FOMO (fear of missing out)? Be thankful for what you have and just sit in that contentment for a few moments now before you head out into your next activity or item on your 'to do' list.

» Be mindful today to stop any wishful thinking that may come up around other people's situations. You are not them and you are not meant to be like them; enjoy who you are. Perhaps set your phone alarm for a few times today to remind you to stop and remember to be content.

DAY 14 » **Compassionate**

Dictionary definitions:

'Compassionate: showing compassion.'
  Collins English Dictionary

'Compassion: a strong feeling of sympathy and sadness for the suffering or bad luck of others and a wish to help them.'
  Collins English Dictionary

Quotes:

'If you want others to be happy, practise compassion. If you want to be happy, practise compassion.'
  Dalai Lama, Tibetan spiritual leader

'The whole idea of compassion is based on a keen awareness of the interdependence of all these living beings, which are all part of one another, and all involved in one another.'
  Thomas Merton, American Trappist monk

'Compassion is not a relationship between the healer and the wounded. It's a relationship between equals. Only when we know our own darkness well can we be present with the darkness of others. Compassion becomes real when we recognize our shared humanity.'
  Pema Chödrön, American–Tibetan Buddhist

'Compassion is an action word with no boundaries.'
  Prince, American singer-songwriter

Insights

If I had to choose one characteristic of leadership to focus on above all others, then being a compassionate person would be top of my list, because I am reminded every day in this troubled world that I could do with more compassion. Compassion interconnects with all the other 49 characteristics we will be looking at in these pages. In particular, a deeper knowledge of connectivity with others is essential if we are to feel and demonstrate compassion.

I remember speaking at a Chamber of Commerce event in Worcestershire in 2018, where I was exploring some of the material within my first book, *Forces for Good*. I was talking about the need for business leaders to consider others in the world with their decision-making around their environmental policies, and for the need for us to realise that all humans are interconnected. One of my slides was a picture of around 100 Bangladeshis wading through waist-deep water, having been flooded out of their homes – a direct consequence in that low-lying country of climate change. As I clicked the slide onto the screen, I could feel emotion welling up and was unable to speak for the next couple of minutes. It was embarrassing at the time, as I wasn't used to crying during presentations at that time, but the impact on the room was profound. That was the first time I had felt such emotion about the suffering of others due to climate change and whenever I used that slide for the next two years, the same thing happened.

Due to this personal growth in compassion, as a company we have been far more proactive in our efforts to reduce our environmental impact. It may be worth noting here the difference between empathy and compassion, which of course, work together. Empathy is about connecting with the emotions of another individual and feeling what they feel; but empathy is a relatively passive state and doesn't require action. Compassion, on the other hand, compels us to act to alleviate the sufferings of others. In my own example here, the connection with the homeless Bangladeshis powerfully propelled me as a leader to change the way we behaved as a company and it kick-started our journey to carbon neutrality, which followed a year later.

There is, of course, a close connection between empathy and compassion. In *An Open Heart* (2002) the Dalai Lama says that the first step to a compassionate heart is empathy and closeness to others:

> The closer we are to a person, the more unbearable we find that person's suffering. The closeness I speak of is not

a physical proximity, nor need it be an emotional one. It is a feeling of responsibility, of concern, of concern for a person.

Some call this interdependence, knowing that as living beings, we are interconnected with all other living beings on the planet. Our actions impact them and their actions impact us – and we will be looking at this on Day 29.

The real impact of that experience at the Chamber of Commerce was due to my having an insight into the suffering of others. Originating from Latin, the word 'compassion' literally means 'a suffering with another'. It is about feeling what they feel and being upset because they are in physical or emotional pain. I have mentioned emotions and it is difficult to imagine true compassion without an emotional element. And, indeed, that emotional element can help spur us into action, as I have described above. Compassion without action is a paradox; as Prince said: 'Compassion is an action word.' In his book *Descartes' Error*, neuroscientist Antonio Damasio shows scientifically how the limbic part of the brain, which is closely linked with our emotions, is a strong factor in our decision making. This is easy for us to understand, as we can probably all remember a time when we have been stirred up by a speaker or seen something in a magazine or on social media that caused us to have an emotional response, leading us to take some form of action. Unless there is action, then, no doubt, our compassion will be diminished; and if we are going to be called compassionate leaders, others need to witness our actions – not just our tears.

A theme we will return to again and again in this book is that by reaching out to others, we significantly increase our own happiness and contentment. There is a sense in the West that if we don't look after ourselves and sort out our own happiness first, then we will somehow be less happy. The reverse is true. As we reach out to others with compassion and put ourselves last not first, we increase our own happiness. As the Dalai Lama says, 'If you want to be happy, practise compassion.' To practise it means compassion in action. Many people all over the world discovered this during the Covid-19 pandemic in 2020. Many more of us were reaching out to others in our communities and cities, and discovering that we increased our own happiness by doing so. It is no coincidence that several of the religions of the East, notably Buddhism and Hinduism, talk a lot about compassion and it is no coincidence that in these regions there is a more highly developed sense of community.

Of course, compassion is not just to be practised towards those we don't know, but also those close to us. Entering into their sufferings as if these were our own will help us to be better mothers, fathers, sisters, brothers, etc... In fact, some, coming from a family at the lower end of the emotional spectrum, may find it most challenging to practise compassion with those close to us. I have met those who find themselves crying at the end of a film or even during an episode of *Britain's Got Talent*, but who find it difficult to engage with those they love with enough compassion. It's not uncommon in our society, but don't worry – compassion will start to flow more easily once we begin to practise it a little more during our periods of reflection and meditation.

During the past fifty years, leaders who have operated with high levels of compassion have stood out as being different, as there are so few of them; but if there is one characteristic that leaders need more than any other in this third decade of the 21st century, it is compassion. Are you ready for the challenge?

Actions

Every day is an opportunity to practise compassion:

» Find a picture in a magazine or online of people who are less fortunate than yourself. Imagine that you are them, feeling what they are feeling and longing for what they long for, and try to connect yourself with their suffering.

» Next, imagine someone you know but don't particularly like. Think good thoughts or pray for them, if you are that way inclined. Hope for good things for them.

» During the day, reach out with compassion to someone who may need some love at work or at the shops or at the school gate. As we actively practise compassion, the feelings will flow too.

DAY 15 » **Courageous**

Dictionary definition:

'The quality of mind or spirit that enables a person to face difficulty, danger, pain, etc., without fear; bravery.'
Dictionary.com

Quotes:

'One isn't necessarily born with courage, but one is born with potential. Without courage, we cannot practice any other virtue with consistency. We can't be kind, true, merciful, generous, or honest.'
Maya Angelou, American poet and political activist

'He who is not courageous enough to take risks will accomplish nothing in life.'
Muhammad Ali, American boxer and activist

'Your time is limited, so don't waste it living someone else's life. Don't be trapped by dogma – which is living with the results of other people's thinking. Don't let the noise of other people's opinions drown out your own inner voice. And most important, have the courage to follow your own heart and intuition.'
Steve Jobs, American entrepreneur.

'Life shrinks or expands in proportion to one's courage.'
Anaïs Nin, French-Cuban diarist

Insights

'You're nothing but a great big coward,' Dorothy said sternly to the Cowardly Lion when she first met him in the woods with the Scarecrow and the Tin Man. 'You're right. I am a coward. I haven't any courage at all,' replied the Cowardly Lion, with tears running down his cheeks and a trembling voice. I am sure you will all recognise that passage from *The Wizard of Oz*, which amongst other parallels is a story about the three characteristics required for a successful journey: the heart of the Scarecrow, the brains of the Tin Man and the eventual courage of the Lion. The wizard later says to the Cowardly Lion: 'Back where I come from, we have men who are called heroes. Once a year they take their fortitude out of mothballs and they parade it down the main street and they have no more courage than you have.' This seems to help the Cowardly Lion, who shows great courage later in the story, saying, 'All right, I'll go in there for Dorothy. Wicked Witch or no Wicked Witch, guards or no guards, I'll tear them apart. I may not come out of there alive but I'm going in there.'

The Cowardly Lion had an external badge of courage, a medal, but we all know that courage comes from the inside, not the outside. Those who look courageous on the outside are often just as nervous and fearful as everyone else, but they have learned to overcome their fears and operate without the fear paralysing them. Take public speaking, for example: a common fear near the top of many people's lists of things they are frightened of. Those of us who are fairly used to public speaking still have the pounding heart and sweaty hands and occasional feelings of faintness. It's just that we have been there before and know that the world isn't going to end when we climb onto the stage. Overcoming the fear on the first occasion with courage enables the experience to become slightly easier to handle each time thereafter.

Thinking back to the introduction, where I talked about operating in the unconditioned self (i.e. freeing ourselves of the behaviour patterns that we have been conditioned to live within), it requires courage to step away from learned behaviour patterns into a new realm. It is far easier to slip back into old behaviour patterns and far more difficult to step into new ones, but our courage when we do is rewarded by feelings of success as our neurochemicals, such as dopamine, kick in. That is the internal equivalent of the Cowardly Lion's medal.

Of course, it is much easier to have courage and take risks in the workplace if there is a safety net underneath us – and good leadership should provide that safety net. If the people who make mistakes are penalised, the culture of fear that this creates will prevent others from having the courage to take risks – which, in turn, will stifle innovation. So, having courage is also about others trusting and supporting us, which will help us take risks. I am sure the lion in *The Wizard of Oz* would not have shown such courage if he had been on his own; knowing that Dorothy and the others were behind him spurred him on. In fact, the word 'encourage' comes from the idea of giving courage to another or inspiring confidence.

The suffragettes required huge amounts of courage during their campaigns for Votes for Women. They often experienced verbal and physical abuse from passers-by as they distributed their newsletters, delivered speeches and chalked on pavements to announce meetings. Many were put in prison and went on hunger strike for their cause; but knowing that they were part of a larger movement would have helped them find the courage for the brave acts they performed. It's astonishing to think that this movement existed only just over 100 years ago. Believing passionately in a cause inspires courage and acts of bravery; and when there is more passion around, there is also more courage.

I have immense respect for those in the Extinction Rebellion movement, who put their necks on the line in demonstrations on the streets of London and other cities. Their courage comes from their passion to convince the rest of the population about the crisis that faces our planet. Many of the people demonstrating have never done anything like this before; it is their passion that drives them. The movement received huge criticism in 2019 when they blockaded the streets of London; yet looking back, they, together with Greta Thunberg, helped to completely shift the climate change debate. So much so, that by September 2019 the *Financial Times* declared on its front page: 'Capitalism: Time for a Reset'. There will be many battles to come in the death throes of capitalism; and I wonder whether more of us need to have the courage of our convictions and be prepared to stand up for the injustices in the world, even if this means becoming unpopular with our friends, and potentially being arrested and even put in prison as we fight for justice for the people and the planet.

Just like the suffragettes, Extinction Rebellion and, more recently, the Black Lives Matter movement, most social uprisings face the risk of the establishment coming down hard on those leading the charge. Yet more courage will be required by those putting their necks on the line, to see the change required for a more equal world. Some of us think that we can't possibly risk criticism and lose our respectability as a leader, or face losing our position of responsibility, but we may have to sacrifice some of this if we want to see justice in the world. Are our respectability and position more important than that? Those leaders who want to see change may need to forfeit respectability for the sake of that change. Yes, we need the brains of the Tin Man to work out what to do, and we certainly need the heart and passion of the Scarecrow, but we possibly need courage above all in order to be like the Lion, who took risks for his friends.

Actions

We may have to wait to find an opportunity to practise courage, but in the meantime:

» Think of a situation where you could have been more courageous in the past and ask yourself why you lacked the courage to act. Journal anything that comes to mind.

» Challenge yourself to think of areas of action that are currently outside your comfort zone and push yourself to find the courage to make a breakthrough.

» Encourage those who are close to you to operate more courageously and help them to achieve their dreams. As a leader, you can be the safety net for them today.

DAY 16 » **Self-sacrificial**

Dictionary definition:

'Sacrificing of one's interests, desires, etc. as for duty or the good of another.'
Dictionary.com

Quotes:

'There is no part of my life, upon which I can look back without pain.'
Florence Nightingale, English social reformer and founder of modern nursing

'There is no success without sacrifice. If you succeed without sacrifice it is because someone has suffered before you. If you sacrifice without success it is because someone will succeed after.'
Adoniram Judson, American missionary

'Great achievement is usually born of great sacrifice and is never the result of selfishness.'
Napoleon Hill, American author

'Life becomes harder for us when we live for others, but it also becomes richer and happier.'
Albert Schweitzer, Alsatian-German polymath

Insights

There have been many amazing stories of self-sacrifice to come out of the tragedy of 9/11, but none more inspiring than that of Richard Rescorla, a British-American Vietnam War vet. On 11 September 2001, he was working as a security director for Morgan Stanley. Hearing of the first plane strike on the North Tower at the World Trade Centre, he calmly instructed some 2,700 employees of Morgan Stanley to evacuate the South Tower – despite an earlier announcement that ordered them to stay at their desks. He ensured everyone for whom he was responsible had left the building before he started to make his own way out. He was still inside the building when it collapsed. Rescorla was declared dead three weeks later, but his body has never been found.

This story is one of numerous amazing tales of self-sacrificial behaviour in adverse circumstances, many of which involve a person laying down their life in the act of the ultimate self-sacrifice. Now, this is something only few of us may ever have to do, yet I'm sure I'm not alone in wondering how I would react in a situation where I had to choose between saving my own life or those of others. Perhaps a slightly morbid daydream, but I believe those individuals who live their lives in a self-sacrificial way would be the first to lay their lives down if it ever came to the big sacrifices. And I hope I would be one of them.

With respect to the day-to-day type of self-sacrifice that we are often called to perform as leaders, most of us didn't have any lectures on this as part of our management training! The Western dream is to live our lives in a moral way, gradually increasing our income, our house size and the value of our car, providing for our families and seeing our children gain a good university education. Nothing wrong with any of that, you may say. However, the myth that many of us have been brought up to believe is that sacrificing our own material dreams is painful in some way, deeply upsetting and reduces our happiness – when actually the very opposite is true. Sacrificing our own gains for others is what leads to greater fulfilment and profound happiness; yet many of us are denied that privilege by the impulse to cling on to what is ours, often through fear, rather than letting it go. In other words, we haven't discovered the great sense of fulfilment that self-sacrifice can bring.

I have talked elsewhere of the ancient wisdom of *ikigai*, a philosophy of life originating in the Japanese island of Okinawa, which has the greatest percentage of centenarians in the world. They believe that people are at their happiest when simultaneously engaging in four core activities:

1. doing something they love
2. doing something they are good at
3. doing something that pays them
4. doing something that the world needs.

Whenever I describe *ikigai*, it resonates with people – particularly those in the corporate world, who realise that some of their own dissatisfaction comes from only doing two or three out of the four activities; and it is often the 'doing something that the world needs' that is left out. A few people have even told me that they left their job after learning more about *ikigai* and are now happier as a result, as they are now doing something that gives out to the world, having sacrificed something to achieve this. Self-sacrifice does indeed bring joy; often it is simply from having the courage to let go of our own insecurities, whether they be financial or otherwise.

There are those who say there is no such thing as altruism or self-sacrifice, and that we have evolved as a species so that anything we do for the good of the wider community is simply in order to earn 'brownie points' for the future, when we might need something from the community in return. While there is some truth in this having been a natural way to strengthen bonds in early human settlements, I would argue that the human soul is capable of more than that – even of sacrifice to the point of death. On a purely physiological level, one of the brain's chemicals, oxytocin, is released whenever we do put others first in some way, and creates those warm fuzzy feelings. All said and done, does it really matter whether we are subconsciously making sacrifices for our mutual benefit and not purely for the benefit of others? We all know those guilty feelings when we don't do the right thing, so who cares? Let's just put others first, it's a win–win!

In the business world, one way of achieving corporate *ikigai* – and therefore more fulfilment for those that work in an organisation – is through a business model that is set up to benefit the world socially or environmentally. Some businesses that do this and subject themselves to a rigorous assessment are known as B Corps. There are now several large companies certifying as B Corps, but sometimes the safety net within such large organisations can unintentionally dampen down the beneficial personal changes that often come through experiencing trials, tribulations and self-sacrifice. No doubt some of the founders of these larger B Corps have experienced degrees of self-sacrifice, but there is often no need for the workers within these organisations to experience their own form of personal sacrifice. As a leader of a B Corp company and an ambassador for the movement, I would want to encourage a self-sacrificial attitude for everybody within these 'good' companies so that the movement doesn't run out of steam.

Many of us, of course, will go through difficult times within our personal lives and are self-sacrificial in ways that others may never know about; and it is certain that self-sacrifice always helps shape us into the sort of compassionate individual who plays an essential part in changing the world. Those of us who have known the joy of self-sacrifice found in serving others must not assume that this attitude is endemic in our organisations and companies. Being the kind of leaders who put their necks on the line in order to do the right thing, deepens us as people and helps us find ourselves; we would do well to encourage everyone to do this and thereby find their own individual deep sense of fulfilment.

Remembering those who are famous for having achieved amazing exploits in their lives, such as Florence Nightingale, it is clear to me that this is very rarely achieved without some level of self-sacrifice. As she said, 'There is no part of my life, upon which I can look back without pain.' These world-changers frequently endure tremendous personal sacrifice and suffering. Their journey often starts with an intention to do the right thing and a sense of feeling powerful enough to achieve this; and as their lives continue, tremendous self-sacrifice is endured. At the same time, they develop a much deeper love and compassion for others, which means they leave an amazing legacy and end their lives with a deep sense of contentment.

Finally, I am reminded of a story I once heard about a farmer whose barn burned down. It had been home to a few chickens. As the farmer was wandering around the scorched remains, he kicked what he thought was a charred ball on the ground. As he did so, four chicks ran out from under it. The ball of burnt feathers was, of course, the mother hen who had laid her life down for her chicks. What a great picture of self-sacrificial leadership.

Actions

So, how can we learn to live a life of greater self-sacrifice:

» Reflect for a few moments as to whether you believe in the myth that excessive material possessions will bring you happiness?

» Ask yourself how much you are prepared to sacrifice yourself for others. Your possessions, your time, your status...? What would you give up for others? Make a list in your journal.

» Think of something you could do today that is self-sacrificial and involves putting another's needs above your own.

DAY 17 » **Joyful**

Dictionary definition:

'Full of joy, as a person or one's heart; glad; delighted.'
Dictionary.com

Quotes:

'When you are joyful, when you say yes to life and have fun and project positivity all around you, you become a sun in the center of every constellation, and people want to be near you.'
Shannon L. Alder, American actress and author

'A joyful heart is the normal result of a heart burning with love. She gives most who gives with joy.'
Mother Teresa, Albanian-Indian missionary

'It makes me sad when I find sisters who aren't joyful. They might smile, but with just a smile they could be flight attendants!'
Pope Francis, Argentinian head of the Catholic Church

'Joy is a sustained sense of wellbeing and internal peace – a connection to what matters.'
Oprah Winfrey, American chat show host

Insights

There's a story I told in my previous book, *Forces for Good*, about a man called Dexter, who was a toll-charge collector on the Golden Gate Bridge across San Francisco Bay. Despite doing a humble job, Dexter always came to work with a smile on his face. More often than not, when motorists stopped by his toll-booth window, he would be singing his favourite songs and laughing as he did so. Whether by his smile, a song or an encouraging word, Dexter would brighten up the day of everyone who passed through his booth to cross the bridge. Those who had started the morning in a bad mood would cross the bridge with a smile on their face and a slightly brighter outlook on the day ahead.

As time went on, something extraordinary started to happen. Often, despite many of the other toll booths having no queue, there would be a long queue at Dexter's booth. Motorists had changed their behaviour in a remarkable way and decided to make their commute slightly longer, just to have their day brightened up by this amazing worker. How extraordinary it was that a man in an unskilled job like this had such a profound influence on people's lives. Sadly, the Golden Gate Bridge now has automated toll booths with no people employed to collect the tolls, but I have no doubt that Dexter's joy is making a positive difference to the world elsewhere. Doesn't the world need more people like Dexter? In fact, the world needs more leaders who lead with joy – it all gets far too serious sometimes, doesn't it?

I am sure we have all met people who are full of joy; even when they are not smiling with their mouth, their eyes seem to smile. Often, they shine like diamonds in a grey world; you may have seen them at the supermarket, on public transport, or, if you are lucky, there may be one in your workplace. We will also be only too aware of those who carry with them the opposite of joy, mood-hoovers I call them, and rather than flocking to be around them, people run a mile from this type of person.

Which type of person are we most comparable to, then? Probably both on different occasions, but when I find myself bringing the atmosphere down a notch, I try to remember to snap out of it quickly before I affect others. I remember to think to myself, 'How dare I be miserable when I am so lucky to do what I do, live where I live and have the variety in my life that I do.' There is, of course, a close connection between being joyful and being thankful, and those who live in gratitude find it difficult not to be joyful. Shannon Alder's quote – about being the sun in every constellation and people wanting to be near you – is absolutely true. People hang around and are attracted to those with joy, as we saw with Dexter's ever-growing queue at the toll booth. So, what exactly is joy? And how can we be full of it?

The trouble with dictionary definitions is that they are occasionally not very helpful. I had to look at five different dictionaries before I found one that expanded on the meaning of joyful as more than 'full of joy'; hence the Dictionary.com entry here, which at least gives us a few more words. But words themselves are sometimes not that helpful either. After all, words are the mere symbols of other dimensions. Is joy happiness? Is joy about contentment? Is joy about thankfulness, which we've already mentioned? Well, yes, it is all those and more. To my mind, there is a depth about joy that isn't present in those other three words. Something deep within us, almost bubbling up like a mountain spring as it emerges out of a rock face, is a good analogy. If, like me, you have ever tried to block such a stream, it is impossible: the water will always find a way out. It is like that for those with joy within them – it will always find a way out, despite the circumstances. Do we think people like Dexter always have a great time at home with their family or on the way to work? Of course not, but they are able to lay anything negative aside and their natural exuberance from deep within bursts forth when they connect with others again.

Each one of our quotes today carries with it a slightly different dimension of these profound words: joy and joyful. Why don't you read them again now? I love Pope Francis's flight attendant analogy, as it carries the sense of the depth of what joy is. A smile can truly be there without the accompanying joy – and we are all too familiar with that. Mother Teresa and Oprah's quotes connect joy to both love and peace; those three words often seem to go together and are frequently seen on Christmas cards. Are these the three qualities that the human soul desires the most, I wonder? Like both love and peace, joy is not something we can develop overnight, but comes through quiet meditation and contemplation, together with a deep sense of self. I once asked someone what they desired most in life, and she said, 'To be happy.' I challenged her by asking how she aimed to find happiness. I'm not sure it works to simply have happiness as a goal, and it is the same with joy. It is by giving out and focusing on loving others that the joy deep within will be brought to the surface. It is simply too difficult to put joy in our internal 'sat nav' and aim for it.

One thing I do know completely is that the words of Eleanor Roosevelt are true, in that 'Comparison is the thief of all joy'. There is no way that we can be continually looking over our shoulders, or more likely looking at our smart phones at what others are doing, and comparing our achievements or happiness with theirs and still remain full of joy. Social media, and the inevitable comparison it brings, is an absolute joy-killer. Much of what we look at is a false impression of other people's highlights. We are meant to be ourselves and doing what we are meant to be, not copying others. Let's learn to be pleased to be ourselves; finding that sort of self-acceptance could just be the start of great joy.

Actions

Let's be full of joy today:

» Let's remind ourselves here to practise gratitude every day. Think of three things to be thankful for now, as thankfulness is the root of joy.

» When you come into a room, do you bring joy with you or something else? Learn to lighten up and focus on bringing a smile to other people's faces today when you walk into a room. Try it today.

» Are you comparing yourself with others too much? If you find yourself doing that today, remind yourself that you are doing what you are meant to be doing – and make that awareness a habit. The joy will start to flow.

DAY 18 » **Vulnerable**

Dictionary definition:

'Someone who is completely and rawly open, unguarded with their heart, mind and soul.'
Urban Dictionary

Quotes:

'Vulnerability is the birthplace of innovation, creativity or change.'
Brené Brown, American professor and author

'To love is to be vulnerable.'
C. S. Lewis, British writer and theologian

'We are called to be fruitful – not successful, not productive, not accomplished. Success comes from strength, stress, and human effort. Fruitfulness comes from vulnerability and the admission of our own weakness.'
Henri Nouwen, Dutch professor, writer, priest and theologian

'When we were children, we used to think that when we were grown-up we would no longer be vulnerable. But to grow up is to accept vulnerability... To be alive is to be vulnerable.'
Madeleine L'Engle, American author

Insights

When I was younger, I used to think that being a good leader was about having strong opinions, certainty and expertise, and confidently driving everyone forward with great assurance. Even when bad stuff was happening, I was there at the front, wearing my confidence mask and looking calm when everything else around me was seemingly falling apart. Now I am older, I realise that all this is only one aspect of leadership, and probably more suited to the captain of a sports team rather than the workplace. Most of us have grown up with a one-sided view of leadership: the masculine side. It's understandable, as much of the leadership we may have experienced during our formative years might have come from men with a very poorly developed feminine side; and it is high time that we got the balance right. Many of the male leaders in the USA and UK are almost caricatures of over-masculinised leadership. Due to this imbalance, many women still feel they have to exhibit these masculine characteristics in order to break through the glass ceiling. So this over-masculinised leadership style has squashed the feminine in both men and women.

Thank God things are changing, albeit too slowly, and leadership characteristics such as vulnerability, inclusivity and empathy are coming to the fore. We will look at empathy and inclusivity on other days, but today, let's explore vulnerability. Yes, there is a place for confidence, which enables those we are leading to feel safe; but there is also a place for weakness and vulnerability in leadership. When I used to exhibit that hyper-masculine style of leadership, I alienated many of those I was leading, particularly women; nor did I look or sound real and authentic. I was an inauthentic version of myself that people couldn't relate to or connect to. A lack of vulnerability meant that I didn't allow myself to show any weakness whatsoever, which in turn meant that I was more difficult to trust and therefore a worse leader than I am today. As I write this, only this morning, my voice started wavering when in a team meeting I read out a poem I had written; the truth is that people can trust and relate to those individuals who show emotions just like they do.

There was a shift for me in learning to be more vulnerable after I was hospitalised with malaria in 2015. There is nothing like being 'blue-lighted' into a hospital and having no memory of the next two days to make you appreciate your own mortality and vulnerability. Just to be clear, at no point was I going to die, but the encounter with my own weakness and realising that I wasn't invincible had an impact on me and my leadership. I now know and express my own vulnerability more; my team are more aware that I am a real human being with feelings; and I certainly don't want to spend any more time living behind a mask. I am not saying the mask is never there and sometimes the right thing to do is to create safety by staying strong for others perhaps when things are falling apart, but it is always important for the real you to shine through whenever possible.

In Brené Brown's quote on page 91, she makes a link between vulnerability and creativity. Many of the best artists are very vulnerable and frequently have crises of confidence. I believe there is a latent creativity within many of us that, for some of us, may be locked up due to our lack of vulnerability. Consider these words of wisdom from Akaya Windwood, President of the Rockwood Leadership Institute:

> Years ago before taking up the work of leading Rockwood, I was an organizational consultant. I was paid to be right – to be an expert. However, as I sit here at my current desk, I realize how very little I really knew about the everyday running of and caring for an organization... The push to provide (and often pretend) expertise when we're really not sure about things can get us into a lot of trouble. It's unhealthy for leaders, because pretending expertise is stressful. It's quite challenging to try and maintain inauthenticity over time. It's unhealthy for our organizations, because if people are feigning skills, it can be difficult to hire the right people into the right positions. It's toxic. So I'm going to coin a new term – Expert Delusional Syndrome, or EDS.

It is this culture of expertise that has prevented many leaders from being vulnerable. It was perhaps easier in the modernist 1960s,'70s and '80s to appear certain, to appear right – and to claim the science would back you up. These days, we can see how everything is changing continually, and it is now OK as a leader to admit you haven't got a clue what is going on. One of my favourite words at present is 'bewilderment', mainly about what is going on in the world. Yes, I sometimes know the direction I think we should travel in, but I feel as vulnerable as everyone else and frightened too sometimes. Leadership is always meant to be collaborative and a room full of experts is never going to make the best decisions. I would prefer anytime a room full of vulnerable people who know they make mistakes every day, rather than a bunch of experts who pretend they don't. As it happens, those who are vulnerable are less likely to make catastrophic errors as they tend to operate collabo-ratively. The 2008 banking crisis was caused by a group of (mainly) men who were not vulnerable (or at least didn't behave like they were), and who didn't communicate with each other properly and weren't honest with each other when everything started to go wrong. Even at that point, much of the damage could have been avoided if they had dropped their masks.

Let's reflect on Henri Nouwen's quote at the start of this chapter, which redefines what success is by calling us to be fruitful through admitting our own weaknesses and vulnerability. It is not the experts, the strong, the accomplished or the productive who will be remembered most fondly at their funerals; it is those who shared their lives, their vulnerabilities and their weaknesses with others in a genuine way. It those who offer other people an honest invitation to see into their lives, warts and all, who will make the best relationships and be the best leaders.

Actions

Learning to be vulnerable is a lifetime's work, but today:

» Reflect for a few minutes on your weaknesses. Remind yourself of what you are not good at. Ask yourself, 'How much of the time do I wear a mask?' Journal anything that comes to mind.

» Try to find an opportunity today to admit to someone a weakness or vulnerability. Let them know you are human!

» Are you guilty of setting yourself up as an 'expert', with all the answers? Go through today and all days being prepared to say, 'I really don't know the answer to that.'

DAY 19 » **Integrous**

Dictionary definitions:

'Integrous: having integrity. Possessing characteristics of honour, valour, loyalty, dedication, and respect.'
Urban Dictionary

'Integrity: Doing the right thing when no-one is looking.'
Urban Dictionary

Quotes:

'The soul is dyed the colour of its thoughts. Think only on those things that are in line with your principles and can bear the light of day. The content of your character is your choice. Day by day, what you choose, what you think, and what you do is who you become. Your integrity is your destiny... it is the light that guides your way.'
Heraclitus, Ancient Greek philosopher

'Real integrity is doing the right thing, knowing that nobody's going to know whether you did it or not.'
Oprah Winfrey, American chat show host

'People with integrity do what they say they are going to do. Others have excuses.'
Laura Schlessinger, American talk show host

'Have the courage to say no. Have the courage to face the truth. Do the right thing because it is right. These are the magic keys to living your life with integrity.'
W. Clement Stone, American businessman and philanthropist

Insights

If you were described as an integrous person, you may wonder whether it was a compliment or not, but it simply means a person full of integrity. I heard the story of a man called James Doty, a neurosurgeon, entrepreneur and university professor, who early in his career was involved in developing the Cyberknife, an invention that netted him millions of dollars. At the turn of the millennium, he promised $30M out of his $75M net worth to charity – just before the dot-com crash of 2000 to 2001, which brought his wealth down to around the $30M he had already pledged. Doty's lawyers advised him that he could renege on his promise and get out of the pledge; surely people would understand the change of circumstances and he wouldn't lose his standing in society. However, Doty was a man of his word and decided to do the right thing and go through with his promise, giving away the last of his fortune to charity.

In a much less costly example, at Cotswold Fayre we announced as a company in the spring of 2019 that we were going to become carbon neutral from August that year; this was based on some logistical changes we had made to vastly reduce the carbon impact of our distribution network, meaning that the carbon offset figure for the carbon used in the distribution of our goods was attainable. The data came from our new logistics company, and either we misunderstood the data at the time or we were just given the wrong figures, but the amount we had to pay to sequester our carbon was considerably higher than what we had budgeted for within the business plan. There was never any doubt within our management team, of course, that we would go ahead and pay the higher amount, even though no one outside the company would know any different. Money doesn't make decisions for us; doing what is right does.

Many companies these days want to link a social purpose to their products and make great claims about the percentage of their profits that they are giving to social justice projects, such as charities working with street children in Brazil. They often push back when I challenge them and ask them how much they have contributed so far; as, of course, many start-up brands don't make any profit for a few years, yet their products may have carried that message for the last two years. To my mind, this approach lacks integrity; surely, it is far better to say that they are going to give 5p for each product sold, for example. In many cases, SMEs can often get away with not doing the right thing, because no one notices what small companies do. That is the great advantage of a certification process such as B Corp, where businesses must provide evidence of what they are doing and be analysed on how good they are for the world: both the people and the planet.

The Urban Dictionary definition of integrity at the top of this chapter is based on a quote often attributed to C. S. Lewis, but which actually paraphrases a line by Charles Marshall: 'Integrity is doing the right thing when no one is watching.' Though I am sure C. S. Lewis would have agreed with the sentiment! It is all too easy these days to trumpet our high moral standing on social media yet then not follow through when the heat is turned up a little. I am concerned that occasionally even well-known ethical companies and their leaders sometimes present a better view to the outside world than what is really happening on the inside of their organisations. There is a need for more integrity and greater depth of character amongst leaders, one of my main motivations for writing this book.

As I have been writing on integrity over this weekend, there has been a huge furore in the Sunday newspapers about the Prime Minister's closest advisor, who is reported to have broken his own rules on the coronavirus lockdown on at least two occasions; and, as I write, he seems completely unrepentant about it. People detest hypocrisy more than absolutely anything in a leader, and it has been the downfall of many political figures. Hypocrisy is also what puts off many people about religions too, which can sometimes appear to have the attitude of 'do what I say, not what I do'. Imagine a stick of Blackpool rock that you can cut through at any point to reveal the word 'Blackpool'. Would people see integrity running through us and our businesses if they were to figuratively cut through us at any point?

The wonderful message from the James Doty story is that even though he 'lost' personally, he still went through with his promises. For some of us, winning is too important and can come at the cost of all else. I know the appeal of this, as, like many entrepreneurs, I am very competitive and hate losing, and I have had to temper that competitive streak to maintain my integrity. There is a great example of this provided by the tennis player Andy Roddick, who was once awarded a match when a second serve from his opponent was deemed to be out. However, Roddick saw the mark in the clay and made the umpire reverse his call. Roddick went on to lose the match but maintain his integrity.

So, how, do we develop our integrity? Well, it is impossible without many of the other characteristics that we will be talking about in this book, such as compassion, faithfulness etc... but probably the most important one is silence. If we speak too hastily and make promises, we are in danger of overpromising and under-delivering. It is best not to speak hastily and to even learn to say 'no' on some occasions, where we risk losing our integrity by disappointing customers, suppliers or, worst of all, team members. One of the most common reasons people leave employers is when they have been promised promotions, money or bonuses that haven't been forthcoming.

In these instances, circumstances may well have changed – as they did for James Doty, to the tune of being $45M poorer; but he stuck with his promises all the same. Incidentally, Doty claimed to be happier than he had ever been after he had given that money away, saying, 'At that moment I realised that the only way that money can bring happiness is to give it away.' Being integrous, or full of integrity, is not only the right thing to do, but we will almost certainly be more fulfilled and happier as a result. Doing the difficult thing or the expensive thing can often make us happier than we expected, due to maintaining our integrity.

Actions

Building integrity is a lifetime's work, but today:

» Reflect on any occasions when you may have looked better on the outside than the inside, and journal about these. Do others see the real you? When you make promises, do you know you will keep them at all costs?

» Perhaps today reinforce to yourself (and maybe others within your team) that you are always going to do the right thing – even if it may be more difficult.

» Does your competitiveness or need to get ahead mean that you break the rules? Remind yourself during the day that acting with integrity equals happiness.

DAY 20 » **Flowing**

Dictionary definition:

> 'Moving in one direction, especially continuously and easily.'
> *Cambridge English Dictionary*

Quotes:

> 'Going with the flow is responding to cues from the universe. When you go with the flow, you're surfing Life force. It's about wakeful trust and total collaboration with what's showing up for you.'
> *Danielle LaPorte, Canadian speaker and entrepreneur*

> 'Flow is being completely involved in an activity for its own sake. The ego falls away. Time flies. Every action, movement, and thought follows inevitably from the previous one, like playing jazz.'
> *Mihaly Csikszentmihalyi, Hungarian psychologist*

> 'Move with the flow. Don't fight the current. Resist nothing. Let life carry you. Don't try to carry it.'
> *Oprah Winfrey, American chat show host*

> 'Flow with whatever is happening and let your mind be free. Stay centred by accepting whatever you are doing. This is the ultimate.'
> *Chuang Tzu, Chinese philosopher*

Insights

The word 'flowing' might appear to be a strange way to describe a leader, but what I am talking about here is about being 'in flow'. If this is a new term for you, allow me to explain how I know when I have been in flow and what it's felt like. One example comes from a game of tennis, when every single shot I tried worked, even some previously impossible ones. I was completely 'in the zone': I was not mentally processing the shots, but simply hitting the ball as I saw it. The person at the other end of the court was exasperated! Unfortunately for my tennis career, those days didn't come along too often; otherwise I would have been a better player and won far more matches.

Another occasion when I absolutely had that flow feeling was during a trip to the North of England a couple of years ago. I had arranged to meet a customer on the way up to a trade event in Harrogate, where I had various meetings before going on to enjoy a meal out with an old friend in Durham that evening. The following day, I met up for coffee with some other friends in the Lake District and stopped off for an evening meal with my dad on my way back home. There was nothing spectacular about it, yet nothing was forced; I had the right amount of time for each interaction and both received and gave out on each occasion. It was easy, light and enjoyable, just as moving smoothly downstream a river would be – hence the word 'flow'.

I had the pleasure of punting a few times while at Oxford University, and I made sure that if I was trying to impress one of the girls on board the punt, I always took on the downstream part of the journey, leaving the upstream leg to another guy in the group. I had learned from previous experience, as I once had an absolute nightmare when punting upstream as the bow of the boat seemed to have a mind of its own, leading to an unfortunate encounter with the river bank. It is also much easier to leave the pole behind in the river bed when punting upstream. I have even seen one poor chap clinging onto the pole, which was embedded in the riverbed, while his punt travelled on without him!

So, why does life often seem to be more like punting upstream rather than going with the flow of the river? That is probably too complicated a question to answer in this short section, and is likely to involve a lifetime's work, but here are a few pointers. Much of it is to do with knowing our purpose, which I'll be talking about in more detail on Day 30. Aligning our day-to-day tasks with our purpose makes it more likely for us to be in flow, as we are more likely to say 'no' to those tasks or activities that are going to take us out of our purpose and therefore out of flow. Of course, there is a balance here: not everything you do as part of your purpose will be easy and trouble-free, but there will often be a sense of being in the right place at the right time. I remember reading Martin Luther King's biography about one Easter Sunday when he was preparing for a church service. At one point, to the surprise of the other leaders, he suddenly left the room and returned having changed his clothes. He told them that he was going to go to prison rather than to attend the church service. Due to the situation at the time, he knew if he handed himself in to the authorities he would be banged up for a few days, something which he could have avoided for several weeks if he had kept travelling. Again, not the easy option for him, but, no doubt, he was in flow.

For around 20 years, starting as a teenager, I frequently used to have a recurring dream about sitting an important exam and realising I hadn't done any revision whatsoever. Now, this wasn't something I would ever do in real life; being a dedicated student, I would always prepare well for exams, particularly as I often hadn't done enough work prior to the exam season. One day, I was talking to someone else who had the same recurring dream and since then I have discovered it is very common. For me, this was all about learning to go with the flow: I needed to understand that I don't need to have worked everything out in advance, including all the 'what ifs', potential consequences and nuances of everything that may happen in a certain situation. In the dream, it is about trusting my instinct to get me through the 'exams' – as it is about trusting my inner self in life.

To revisit the earlier tennis example, one reason most people don't enter a state of flow in sport is due to overthinking what they are doing with each shot, rather than simply 'feeling' it. The other reason is because they haven't practised enough. Desiring to live more in flow is no excuse for under-preparation. As Regina Brett, American podcaster, has said, 'Over-prepare, then go with the flow.' That is a great way of looking at it, and I try to operate like that when I am speaking in public. I always have more than enough content prepared; however, I never use it all but instead spend longer in certain areas, depending on what I feel the audience is responding to. This is much easier in a face-to-face situation than during webinars, I have discovered, when we were forced to deliver more online content during the Covid lockdown.

Those who overthink and find it difficult to flow are also those who are still learning, just like me, to live constantly in the present moment. It is too easy to be in one conversation, meeting or meal and to be thinking about what's next or recalling an event earlier in the day. This relates to the common Western disease of introspection and over-planning and we can learn from the Eastern gurus much about living in the present. The present moment is sacred to them and as a result many flow beautifully and with fewer wrong diversions through life than we do.

Actions

Let's learn to live in the present and start to flow today:

  » Reflect for a few minutes and look back at the last few days: have you been flowing downstream or trying to punt upstream? What could you do to change this?

  » Be prepared to go off-piste or off-script today at some point. Trust your instincts to do something you wouldn't have risked previously.

  » Set your alarm on your phone today a few times to remind you to stop and remember to live in the present moment.

DAY 21 » **Inclusive**

Dictionary definition:

'Including everyone. Especially: allowing and accommodating people who have historically been excluded (as because of their race, gender, sexuality, or ability).'
Merriam-Webster Dictionary

Quotes:

'It is only human supremacy, which is as unacceptable as racism and sexism, that makes us afraid of being more inclusive.'
Ingrid Newkirk, British animal rights campaigner

'Each human being, however small or weak, has something to bring to humanity. As we start to really get to know others, as we begin to listen to each other's stories, things begin to change. We begin the movement from exclusion to inclusion, from fear to trust, from closedness to openness, from judgment and prejudice to forgiveness and understanding. It is a movement of the heart.'
Jean Vanier, Canadian philosopher and theologian

'The diversity in the human family should be the cause of love and harmony, as it is in music where many different notes blend together in the making of a perfect chord.'
'Abdu'l-Bahá, former head of the Baha'i Faith

'Difference between diversity and inclusion is being invited to a house and being able to rearrange the furniture.'
Jane Silber, American businessperson

Insights

As a white, heterosexual male, I didn't feel qualified to write this chapter on my own with any integrity, so I asked for help and am indebted to Earl Lynch, an expert in 'unconscious bias', for helping me with the material here. Those who have been excluded due to their gender, sexuality, skin colour or disability need to be listened to far more than me. Remember, if you will, a time from your own past when you were upset to be left out of an event, a party or a trip out with people you thought were friends: that feeling you're experiencing right now reflects in a very small way how others feel for whom being excluded is a normal, everyday occurrence. Alternatively, remember a time when you felt you should have won an award or a promotion and were looked over, and someone less deserving than you won what you felt should have been yours? Unfortunately this is an everyday event for many. The difference being is that they are left out because of something they can't change – their skin colour, for example – whereas you may have missed out on that award due to your ability.

Exclusivity is vile, yet we are currently living in a society, certainly in the UK and USA, that seems to be making some progress one year and then going backwards the following year. (I originally wrote this section before the Black Lives Matter movement made the headlines; maybe this time, real progress will be made. Please let that be true.) Any society is only as strong as its weakest members, and progress in this area benefits everyone. When I lived in Deptford, southeast London, I read up on some of the local history and was surprised to discover that the famous diarist Samuel Pepys would have been a neighbour of mine in the 17th century. I was even more surprised to read that Peter the Great of Russia stayed with Pepys on an incognito trip across Europe in the late 17th century. The aim of his trip was to understand more of the world outside Russia, and he was amazed by the commercial success of Holland, a tiny nation that was as prosperous as Russia. One factor, he concluded, was the inclusive nature of society that was encouraged in Holland at the time. In a time when the Catholic Church was declaring that there was no salvation possible for those outside the Church, the Dutch nation operated in the opposite spirit and turned a blind eye to any differences, treating different types of people as equals, which Peter the Great thought led to the country's economic success.

We live in a world that is becoming increasingly unequal, with power and wealth being concentrated in fewer people's hands than ever before. It is in these largely white males' interest to keep society as it is.

Why create a world that is more inclusive if it means they will lose some of their power? In *The Spirit Level*, Richard Wilkinson and Kate Pickett clearly and scientifically demonstrate that a more equal society is better for everyone: the poor are happier, which may not be unexpected, but so are the more affluent. Inclusivity of opportunity – whatever a person's sexuality, gender, skin colour or disability – is better for the dominant and powerful too. This same principle is true at a company level as well. If some people within a business do not feel they have the same opportunities as others, then everyone in that company or organisation will be less fulfilled and happy. So how do we become truly inclusive as a leader? What and how can we change?

Being inclusive is about empathy; it is about understanding how others, who may be different to us, are feeling. We assume the minorities in our workplace are happy because they turn up every day. This is not necessarily true; they come to work to earn money and they may as well come to your business than elsewhere. A well-respected organisation with inclusivity embedded within its culture (or so they thought) surveyed its people and found that their non-whites did not enjoy coming to work as much as their white employees. They were shocked as this went against their whole ethos, so they started to examine themselves and allow the minority groups to change them from within. Without the correct information we have no hope of being inclusive.

My favourite quote of the four I have included today is that from Jane Silber, a board member of Canonical, which was formed to support the open-source software Ubuntu. In it, Silber talks about the important difference between diversity and inclusion. We may have patted ourselves on the back for having a diversity policy, but certainly have not let others rearrange our rather institutionalised furniture. We must investigate our blind spots and find out from those from whom we haven't previously made an effort to hear, and ask ourselves why they haven't been given permission to change the organisations and companies for which they work.

One clear indication that you haven't built an inclusive organisation as a leader is when everyone agrees with you most of the time. Inclusive companies have plenty of disagreements within them, as absolutely everyone has permission to speak out and say how things feel from their perspective, which is guaranteed to be different to yours. As a leader, you are not always right!

Reaching out to others is something we'll reflect upon in the 'hospitality' chapter and it is essential here too. We must connect with those people who are not the loudest people in the room in order to understand how we have taken opportunity away from them; otherwise we will never be able to do anything about their plight, and we will never be truly inclusive. Just as it would be a paradox to describe ourselves as humble, it is only the people not like us within our companies and organisations who should be given permission to describe us as inclusive. When some voices within our businesses, communities or nations are not free to express themselves fully, we are all weaker for the missing notes, to use one of the founders of the Baha'i Faith 'Abdu'l-Bahá's imagery here. Imagine the huge noise made by an orchestra in the dramatic finale of a symphony: it is our job as the conductor-leader to ensure every instrument is heard, from the bassoon to the piccolo, for the full impact of the orchestra. It is that powerful noise, which if you are listening live, you can feel in your whole body and shakes that room in a way that a few strings or wind instruments can never do on their own. In fact, far too often our businesses and organisations have sounded several instruments short of a good orchestra. It is only by practising complete inclusivity that the full potential of a company or organisation will be achieved within the world.

Actions

What you do today will depend on who you are, and whether you have been the powerful or the disempowered, but first:

» Remember back to a time in your life when you have felt excluded and remember how that felt. Think of those you know who may be feeling like that now and resolve to be someone who makes a difference.

» Look for opportunities today to listen and find out if there is 'unconscious bias' within your company or organisation. What are you going to do about it?

» Why not schedule a survey within your company or organisation to determine how included everyone feels and to reveal your organisation's blind spots?

DAY 22 » **Anonymous**

Dictionary definition:

> 'Made or done by someone whose name is not known or not made public.'
> *Cambridge English Dictionary*

Quotes:

> 'I was born out of due time in the sense that by temperament and talent I should have been more suited for the life of a small Bach, living in anonymity and composing regularly for an established service and for God.'
> *Igor Stravinsky, Russian composer and conductor*

> 'In a nation of celebrity worshipers, amid followers of the cult of personality, individual modesty becomes a heroic quality. I find heroism in the acceptance of anonymity, in the studied resistance to the normal American tropism toward the limelight.'
> *Shana Alexander, American journalist*

> 'Anonymity is not necessarily something to shun; we don't have to achieve celebrity to make a mark on the world.'
> *Mal Fletcher, Australian futurist and commentator*

> 'Many of the bravest never are known, and get no praise. [But] that does not lessen their beauty...'
> *Louisa May Alcott, American novelist*

Insights

You may think that 'anonymous' is one of the more unusual characteristics of leadership to be reflecting upon, but I am really talking about a diminishing of the ego, and letting go of the need to be in the limelight and to be important in other people's eyes. Of course, there may always be part of us that likes to be recognised for the good we do, but it is a virtue to be equally comfortable with not gaining any recognition and to be happy simply knowing we are doing the right thing. For some leaders, it is too important to be the hero of the hour. A key characteristic of good leadership is to be able to lead in such a way that others receive praise, sometimes undeservedly, yet not minding at all as a greater purpose is being served. There are times when leadership is about being strong and being the figurehead and protector of your team, but there are probably more occasions when it is about enabling others to become empowered leaders themselves.

In his book, *Mandela's Way*, Richard Stengel tells the story of being out walking with Nelson Mandela early one morning when Mandela began to reminisce about herding cattle. Now, anyone who has been to Africa will know that it is a common sight to see very young boys out with these large animals, leading them to different grazing areas on common land. Stengel recalls how Mandela had this experience as a young boy:

> 'You know, when you want to get the cattle to move in a certain direction, you stand at the back with a stick, and then you get a few of the cleverer cattle to go to the front and move in the direction that you want them to go. The rest of the cattle follow the few more energetic cattle in the front, but you are really guiding them from the back.' He paused. 'That is how a leader should do his work.'

Later, when talking about Mandela's experience of being brought up by a tribal king, Stengel says:

> A good chief does not grandly state his opinion and command others to follow him. He listens, he summarizes, and then he seeks to mould opinion and steer people towards an action, not unlike the young boy herding cattle from the back of the herd. Mandela regards this as the best of the African tradition of leadership. He sees the West as the bastion of personal ambition, where people fight to get ahead and leave others

behind... The African model of leadership is better expressed as *ubuntu*, the idea that people are empowered by other people, that we become our best selves through unselfish interaction with others.

Those beautiful words sum up much of what I want to say about anonymity and probably also remind us of the opposite – of the poor examples of leadership we have seen in the past. Hopefully they will spur us on to being that selfless, anonymous leader, who loves it when those they lead come to their own conclusions and stride out confidently, leading others, albeit with the safety net of knowing that we are behind them.

I baulk a little when I am described by others as the owner of Cotswold Fayre, and while, for now, I still own a majority of shares, I am keen for everyone else who works there to feel a sense of ownership; in fact, the plan is to gradually release more and more shares to the rest of the team to help encourage that sense of ownership. I have always said, partly in jest but also with some truth, that my main growth strategy was to always ensure I went on plenty of holidays. That way, in the early days, people made decisions and didn't have to refer to me all the time. Then when I came back from holiday, I let them carry on as they had done such a good job without me. Yes, leadership is about protection and creating a feeling of safety, but it is also about trusting and releasing.

I mentioned in the chapter on humility that Gandhi always used to travel around India in third-class carriages on trains and because there was very little photography in those days, no one knew what he looked like; which led to him being treated as a 'normal' person – so sometimes badly. There was no sense of 'Do you know who I am?' with him. A more modern leader, who I would love to have met, was the co-founder of Southwest Airlines, Herb Kelleher, who *Fortune* magazine called 'the best CEO in America'. Yet Herb always chose to have one of the offices without windows in the organisation's HQ building. I have read in several places, including in *Forbes* magazine, that Herb felt it was important to set an example to the rest of the company by deliberately not choosing the best office as the CEO of the company. He was a great believer that the team was far more important than the individual, which was foundational to the egalitarian nature of the airline. In case you are wondering who got the room with the best view in their HQ, it was everyone – because the cafeteria looked out over the runway.

There is a huge amount of nonsense that goes on within business with regards to status – and we have all seen it. The chauffeur-driven

Rolls-Royce that collects the latest winner of the BBC's *The Apprentice* hardly sends out the right message to a young upcoming business leader, does it? As I have mentioned elsewhere, we have some rewriting of our leadership code yet to do. Too much of the leadership we have endured over the years has been masculine in style, both from men and sadly, also women, who through no fault of their own have had to sometimes behave like men to push through the blockages to their career. Strong, noisy and status-driven, the masculine needs tempering by more feminine qualities, such as compassion, empathy and collaboration – and I would include anonymity here too. There is a comfort and peace about leading from the background, a pride in seeing those we lead receive acclamation and praise, and a sense of excitement about seeing those that we are leading going on up ahead of us.

Maybe it is time for us to renounce the need to be recognised, the need to win awards and the need to be written about in magazines and online? I mention it as someone who has probably wanted that recognition too much in the past. As Mal Fletcher, the futurist and speaker, says, 'We don't need to become a celebrity to make a mark on the world.' In fact, there are many millions of people doing just that, quietly, anonymously and without recognition. Are you willing to join them?

Actions

Today, let's quietly go about our day in the spirit of anonymity:

» Reflect for a while on whether you have wanted recognition or the limelight for your own ego's requirements. Relinquish that need quietly now.

» How good are you at leading from the back? Do you empower others to go ahead of you and take the praise, even when it is perhaps not due?

» Set an alarm three times during the day to ask yourself this question: Am I happy for the purpose to be served without demanding recognition for myself?

DAY 23 » **Available**

Dictionary definition:

'Obtainable or accessible; capable of being made use of; at hand.'
Collins English Dictionary

Quotes:

'There are a lot of people who will give money or materials, but very few who will give time and affection.'
Daniel Keyes, American author

'Attention is the rarest and purest form of generosity.'
Simone Weil, French philosopher and mystic

'If friendship is to transpire between two people, it is important that both be in a state of availability.'
Ignace Lepp, French writer

'If you are capable, but not available, nature will raise a person with lesser ability to replace you soon.'
Israelmore Ayivor, Ghanaian writer and speaker

Insights

I have occasionally visited the Northumbria Community near Berwick-up-on-Tweed, a group who base their life together on the Celtic saints of the first millennium. The community has two rules of life: vulnerability and availability. Of course, the two go together; availability with no emotional vulnerability is not real availability. So here I am talking about both emotional availability (quality) and physical availability (quantity), or, in other words, being generous with our time.

A long time ago, our company was being assessed for the Investors in People standard, and the examiner noted how impressed he was by my managerial 'open-door policy'. I didn't tell him that we didn't have a policy, but it was common sense to me that any one of the 20 or so colleagues in the business at that time could come and talk to me whenever they needed to, even if I wasn't their line manager. Visiting other businesses where the owners and directors are locked away in separate offices seems very strange to me; if you are there physically, then make yourself available to people. Yes, we all need time and space to concentrate on our work from time to time, but that can always be done away from the hours when others are likely to want to talk to you. If you are at the office or even working remotely, then being available physically is important to your people.

So simply being available is one aspect, but that may not be enough of a prompt if people have come from another business culture or, indeed, another manager's culture within your own organisation. How do we make ourselves visibly available? Some will assume you have barriers up around you even if they aren't there, so there is often a need to signal your availability to your colleagues. According to Robert Murdock in a paper called 'Radical Availability', it is important to 'show clear signals of your availability, and actively reinforce the idea that reaching out will be rewarded. It is very easy to set up invisible barriers, and a big part of being available is to actively dismantle barriers around yourself.' In other words, it is no good just having an open-door policy: people need to know that they are metaphorically welcome to step right into the kitchen and make themselves a cup of tea, or, better still, have you make it for them.

Throughout this book, I have talked about clearing our minds of old, outdated ideas of leadership and trying to supplant them with the right ideas. When it comes to leadership, too often we have in our minds the image of a state leader who is flanked by armed bodyguards and who is kept apart by physical barriers from anyone other than his inner circle;

whereas a much better picture of true leadership is the image of Mother Teresa crouching next to a poor, hungry soul in India. If you think back to a time when someone you perceived as more important than you took the time to talk to you, then you know how special that felt. Today's leaders know they have a problem, because if they are not seen as 'available' and at street level, they know that their people find it more difficult to trust them; so many larger companies have now removed their directors' dining area and senior staff now mix with everyone else in the general canteen. The same is true of prime ministers wanting to be seen to be 'of the people' so they engage in normal activities such as cycling to work – something that David Cameron did, which worked well until people found out that his chauffeur-driven car containing his briefcase was following behind him.

To be truly available also means engaging people with your full attention and hearing what they are saying with both their words and non-audible cues; some call this active listening. People are empowered when they know they are really being listened to. How do we do it? First, put down or even better switch off your phone, and give the person your full attention by orientating yourself so you are face on to them, with full eye contact. Next, show that you are listening by nodding where appropriate to affirm what they are saying and then repeat back to them what you have heard them say, to show them that you understand. Continue to give them your full attention and do not start thinking of a response until after they have finished talking. When the moment comes, respond to them appropriately without judging what they have said. You may have a different opinion to them, but their opinion reflects exactly how they see the situation and as such is perfectly valid. Active listening is part of being available to others and builds trust like nothing else.

It is a shame that after a decade or so of smart phones, many people have lost the art of listening properly due to our increasingly short attention spans; we are often distracted by wondering about the notifications in our pocket while we are talking to someone else. Being available means the phone comes a distant second to real people, and this applies both in the work environment and home. I absolutely love holidays or short breaks with my wife as there is space to connect with each other, with nothing else in the way. When we are out for dinner in the evening I often leave my phone in the hotel room, so I continue to be amazed when we are eating out in an idyllic setting, with the waves crashing nearby, and I look around the restaurant to see couples completely individually engrossed in their phones. One day I hope people will wake up to one another again.

We talked about invisible barriers earlier when discussing physical availability, and there can also be barriers of trust to be broken down if we are to engage fully with others within our organisation or, indeed, family. A level of openness and transparency is required for others to feel that you are fully available to them. For example, if they believe that you as a leader are privy to lots of information about their team or the company in general that they are not aware of, then that will limit their trust in you. I believe in complete transparency within the workplace: our revenue and P & L figures are displayed in public view on the main whiteboard and we share both good and bad news with the team. Sometimes we may choose the time at which we share the news, but nothing is secret for too long. When you treat people as grown-ups and share information, they will feel connected and engaged, and see you as being fully available.

Actions

Learn to be available today:

» First, reflect on how available as a leader you are to your work colleagues, both physically and emotionally. What could you do to increase your accessibility? Journal anything that comes to mind.

» If you live with others – or, if not, think of your friends – how available are you to them on a personal level? To what degree could you be more open and honest?

» Try active listening today in at least one of your conversations. If this is new to you, you may find it helpful to write down the steps I have outlined above as a memory jogger.

DAY 24 » **Patient**

Dictionary definition:

'Bearing provocation, annoyance, misfortune, delay, hardship, pain etc., with fortitude and calm and without complaint, anger or the like.'
Dictionary.com

Quotes:

'Patience is waiting. Not passively waiting. That is laziness. But to keep going when the going is hard and slow – that is patience. The two most powerful warriors are patience and time.'
Leo Tolstoy, Russian author

'Have patience with all things, but chiefly have patience with yourself. Do not lose courage in considering your own imperfections but instantly set about remedying them – every day begin the task anew.'
Saint Francis de Sales, French bishop and saint

'Patience is not just about waiting for something... it's about how you wait, or your attitude while waiting.'
Joyce Meyer, American minister

'There is something good in all seeming failures. You are not to see that now. Time will reveal it. Be patient.'
Swami Sivananda, Indian spiritual teacher

Insights

There is an ancient Chinese parable about a farmer who planted bamboo seeds, hoping to provide for his family for years to come with the money he could obtain through selling the crop. He planted the seeds and carried water in buckets every day to water them. Initially he didn't expect to see any growth, but after a year he was hoping to see some shoots. However, there was absolutely nothing. He faithfully continued watering the area where he had planted the seeds for another year; still absolutely nothing had happened. He began to become frustrated but patiently continued to water the area for a third year. The other villagers were laughing at him and mocking him by now, as he still had no rewards to show from three years of the hard work of carrying water to the plot every day. A fourth year went by and still there was nothing showing above the ground. The farmer was, by now, becoming extremely frustrated and not a little depressed, but he said to himself, 'I can't stop now.'

One day though, in the fifth year, the whole village was awoken by the farmer shouting and cheering, as he could see some small shoots coming out of the ground. The shoots were almost growing in front of his eyes and quickly grew to a metre, then 2 metres and in six weeks they had grown to an astonishing 25 metres tall. This parable is, of course, about us and our growth and maturity and having the patience to see success after many years of supposedly fruitless watering. But what was going on during those first four years? An incredible root system was developing under the soil, which could sustain the incredibly water-demanding growth of the bamboo plant once it emerged from the ground. If the farmer had poked around under the soil, he would have ruined this development and the bamboo would not have grown.

It is just like this with us. We live in an instant, quick-fix society and often do not have the patience to see projects through to the long-term positive outcome. Inevitably, as I write each chapter of this book, I am examining myself as to how I measure up with each particular attribute, and while I can feel I have made good progress in some, I am not sure I have done so in the area of patience. I left university wanting to join a charity-based project immediately and make a positive impact somewhere in the world, but to my initial disappointment, I found myself driving a lorry for six months and then spent three years in sales. If I had understood patience, I would have had greater appreciation for the vital lessons I was learning about life and business during those years, which have stood me in good stead ever since.

Consider the patience that someone like Gandhi had to endure: he wanted to see justice in his own land, but spent many years in the 'wrong' country of South Africa before returning to India to make a revolutionary difference there. Or indeed, Nelson Mandela, who was in the right country but unfortunately locked away in prison for 27 years, making his dream of establishing equality for all people, whatever their skin colour, unachievable while he was locked away. Yet, just like the story of the bamboo plants, preparation was going on in the characters of these men, while they were supposedly in the wrong place. They both achieved far more in a much shorter time afterwards and speedily fulfilled their vision, largely due to the years of patient character building.

If we revisit the Joyce Meyer quote on page 115, she is talking not just about the waiting, but our attitude while we are waiting. Some of us have learned a little about the waiting, but still have much to learn about the attitude. Quite often we can look calm and patient on the outside, but underneath we are frustrated and slightly grumpy. The long dictionary definition of 'patient' quoted earlier offers a formidable list of what we must withstand to demonstrate true patience, doesn't it?

Another word we could have used is 'stickability', the ability to persevere when circumstances might be opposing you. Many successful people have had to put up with financial hardship, others criticising their actions or telling them it will never work and yet more letting them down on their promises. Ask any successful person and I guarantee they will have experienced some or all of that. The less patient of us give up and move on to something else, but those who are sure that they are following their dreams will keep going and succeed. These people are sure of their purpose and have faith that, in the end, they will prevail. In the words of St Francis de Sales they 'have patience with themselves'. Sometimes we just need to relax into the fact that what we hope for often takes longer than we want or expect.

We have talked mainly so far of the characteristic of patience with respect to a long-term project, but what about patience on a day-to-day basis? The trouble with entrepreneurial types and leaders is that we can sometimes project our impatience with ourselves onto others. We want to see that task completed tomorrow, which we may be able to do if we stay up all night. Others may take a little longer and will probably do a better job than us anyway, as they pay more attention to detail. Part of empowering others is not about breathing down their necks but allowing them to complete jobs in their own way and in their own time, and to let them make mistakes and learn from them. Impatiently jumping in halfway through will stop them from learning and eventually stunt their growth.

While writing this section, I've been watching our cat, Tom, who has been sitting on the edge of the pond for at least two hours, looking at the fish, patiently hoping that he can make a catch. He has been sitting there on sunny days for more than five years and still hasn't succeeded, but maybe one day... Do we have the patience of a cat too?

Actions

Let's learn to be a little more patient today:

» Reflect on someone you know, or someone you know about, who is more patient than you. In a few quiet moments, pay respect to and learn from their patience.

» Think back to a time when you have given up on a dream and not been patient enough. Have you learned from that? Do you need to go back to following that dream?

» In terms of everyday life at work or home, think today how you can be more patient and give others space and time to talk and learn. Make some notes on the areas in which you could be more patient.

DAY 25 » **Hospitable**

Dictionary definition:

> 'Receiving or treating guests or strangers warmly and generously.'
> *Dictionary.com*

Quotes:

> 'A brother came to a hermit: and as he was taking his leave, he said, "Forgive me, Abba, for preventing you from keeping your rule." The hermit answered, "My rule is to welcome you with hospitality, and to send you on your way in peace."'
> *Anonymous, from the Desert Fathers and Mothers*

> 'Hospitality, therefore, means primarily the creation of a free space where the stranger can enter and become a friend instead of an enemy. Hospitality is not to change people, but to offer them space where change can take place...'
> *Henri Nouwen, Dutch professor, writer, priest and theologian*

> 'Hospitality means we take people into the space that is our lives and our minds and our hearts and our work and our efforts. Hospitality is the way we come out of ourselves. It is the first step towards dismantling the barriers of the world. Hospitality is the way we turn a prejudiced world around, one heart at a time.'
> *Joan D. Chittister, American Benedictine nun*

> 'Hospitality is present when something happens for you. It is absent when something happens to you. Those two simple prepositions – for and to – express it all.'
> *Danny Meyer, American restaurateur*

Insights

To my mind, two factors are essential to true hospitality: non-reciprocity and food. Let's tackle the second one first, before becoming a little more philosophical with the first. Food and drink are a good indication of a country's culture and how they are served is absolutely wrapped up in a nation's understanding of hospitality. 'Welcome' and 'love' are two words that are impossible to understand in many cultures without there being food and drink present. In fact, we need to remember that, yet again, our practice of inviting someone in for a cup of tea might seem hospitable, but in many cultures this would be rude, as any welcome into a home would always involve a meal. If we claim that our work and business is about relationships, then I would challenge us all to include more food and drink in our meetings. Welcoming people to our meals and into our homes is perhaps strange within a work context in our culture, but it is odd not to do so in other cultures. There something transformative about eating with others, as the following story shows.

I remember, many years ago, being stuck on the Greek island of Serifos one April, just before the tourist season started, because I hadn't realised there were only two boats from the island a week. The island is only five by five miles and there wasn't much to do, but we managed to find a motorbike to ride over to the other side of the island where there was a convent occupied by a solitary nun. Without giving notice, we arrived at the convent around lunchtime and, to our amazement, the nun cooked us an amazing meal, and without any language in common we somehow managed to converse for two hours. There was a connection with her due to her wonderful hospitality – food and love offered with no strings attached.

On another occasion, while travelling across the Taklamakan Desert, I was invited into the home of a Muslim family in the middle of nowhere. A group of us had been travelling with sand as our only view for more than twelve hours, yet in this completely out of the way place I connected with the man of the house through his hospitality. How they managed to produce a meal like that in the middle of a desert is still a mystery. Yet the same combination of food and a welcome into someone's home created a connection not possible without a meal. It was both amazing and humbling at the same time. Hospitality is perhaps more incredible when in a very poor part of the world, where people will always ensure you receive the best meal they have had for at least a week. Perhaps they will offer you chicken, which they only usually eat once a week; and on one occasion we were served goat, which our hosts would only kill twice a year or so. There is a large part of you that really doesn't want this special treatment, but to deprive people of the opportunity to show hospitality would be rude and very unloving. I have always been personally challenged when receiving this level of hospitality to ask myself, 'Do I show the same to others?'

I love the definition of hospitality by Danny Meyer as being something that is done for us and not to us. It is about creating space where change can take place and, without doubt, many of us need to create more of that kind of space in our lives. There is something here about barriers being removed, vulnerabilities exposed and unconditional love being demonstrated. When all that is happening, it is difficult for change not to occur. In true hospitality there is also non-reciprocity. Some forms of hosting – for example, Western-style dinner parties – are generally not a true demonstration of hospitality. A sense of obligation is often created, as it generates a requirement to return the invitation. I have, in the past, continued to invite people over who have never invited me back, to go in the opposite spirit of the age, but then they become embarrassed and stop accepting!

You know when you are operating in true hospitality when the thought of reciprocity is nowhere near your mind when welcoming people into your home. Just serving food and enjoying their company is enough. The same is true for the guests. Being able to receive without the need for reciprocity can be difficult for many of us. We need to learn to accept the hospitality shown to us, to welcome the love behind it and revel in the friendship that it creates. If we are unable to simply receive hospitality, we run the risk of the sort of free space described by Henri Nouwen not being created.

Perhaps we need to learn even more about showing hospitality to those who will never be able to return it, such as the homeless, the stranger, the struggling single parent or the orphan. There are stories in many cultures of doing good and feeding the weak and those rejected by society. True hospitality is about welcoming them into our hearts and homes and ensuring that they are guests at our feasts. Hospitality is not just about food and drink and welcoming people into our homes though; it is about loving other human beings, even those who may not seem on the surface to be particularly lovable.

And that, for me, is the reason why being hospitable is important for leaders. Yes, it is about food and drink and enjoying the company of others and, yes, it is also about non-reciprocity and there being no strings attached – but it is about more than both of these. Being hospitable is about an attitude of heart. It is about welcoming all others into our lives, whether they are of a different social class, different skin colour or different sexuality. How welcoming are we as people, as leaders? Are there those we wouldn't welcome into our homes to eat and drink with us? Could we truly be called a hospitable leader?

Actions

Let's learn to be hospitable today:

» Reflect for a minute on your own hospitality. How openly do you show hospitality to others with your welcome and an open heart? Do you create space for others with your welcome?

» Is your home open to receiving unexpected guests? How can you be more hospitable within your business or organisation? Journal about some ways that you could demonstrate greater hospitality at home and work.

» Think of someone or a group of people that you can invite to your home, who will be unlikely to invite you back – and send out that invitation this week.

DAY 26 » **Silent**

Dictionary definition:

'Making no utterance: not speaking or making noise.'
Merriam-Webster Dictionary

Quotes:

'We need to find God, and he cannot be found in noise and restlessness. God is the friend of silence. See how nature – trees, flowers, grass – grows in silence; see the stars, the moon and the sun, how they move in silence... We need silence to be able to touch souls.'
Mother Teresa, Albanian-Indian missionary

'There is a contemplative in all of us, almost strangled, but still alive, who craves quiet enjoyment of the Now, and longs to touch the seamless garment of silence which makes whole.'
Alan P. Tory, Australian theologian

'He who sits alone and is quiet has escaped from three wars: hearing, speaking, seeing; but there is one thing against which he must continually fight: that is his own heart.'
Antony (Desert Father)

'You are most powerful when you are most silent. People never expect silence. They expect words, motion, defense, offense, back and forth. They expect to leap into the fray. They are ready, fists up, words hanging leaping from their mouths. Silence? No.'
Alison McGhee, American author

Insights

How can a leader be silent, you may be thinking? I don't mean all the time, of course, but I think we would do well to speak less and listen more in many cases, both to our inner voice and to the voices of others. Many of us are surrounded by noise for much of our lives. Even as I sit here writing in my house in the relative quiet of the countryside, I can hear the distant roar of traffic, birds singing and one of my neighbours using a power tool. Some find silence extremely threatening and can't abide to live in quiet. The TV is turned on as soon as they enter the living room, they are constantly wired to music even when exercising and they go to sleep with the radio on. We have talked about solitude already, on Day 6, and while there is some overlap here, it is, of course, possible to be alone and not be silent, and it is possible to be in company and be silent. Here we are reflecting on speaking less or being content in silence and speaking where appropriate. Many of us talk too much.

Most religions in the world have discovered the power of silence and the benefits it can bring; and now some secular groups also organise silent retreats as an antidote to our over-noisy world. My mum went to a Quaker school and I remember her telling me that they had to eat their meals in silence and were not even allowed to ask for condiments such as salt and pepper. Others had to notice that you wanted them and offer them to you. Subconsciously, she carried this through to her adult life and would often sit waiting at the beginning of her meal, longing for the salt that her hungry children hadn't passed to her. Communication can indeed happen in silence and perhaps that is a lesson we need to learn. Many of us will have experienced sitting in a room with someone we love, perfectly comfortable, not having to say anything yet experiencing a depth of communication and connection. Words are superfluous in that sort of situation and silence is only awkward when we don't know others well.

I remember being introduced to the 'poustinia' on a trip to the Northumbria Celtic Community. The word comes from the Russian for desert and in this case the 'desert' was a windowless dark shed containing one hard chair and one small desk with a candle burning on it. As part of my retreat I was to spend an hour in absolute silence in the poustinia, with only a candle for company. If you are not used to it, an hour of silence is a very long time, but it was a profound experience for me, at the time coming from a very activity-centred life with several small children. There is a depth of knowing ourselves through silence which allows us to connect with the world better. I build some silence into every day of my life now, even when I think I don't have time to stop.

The musician John Cage staged a piece called *4'33"* as part of a concert. When the time came for that part of the concert, the orchestra fell silent for 4 minutes, 33 seconds. Cage wanted the audience to hear the sound of silence around them, before listening to the rest of the concert with greater appreciation. The same is true for us in conversations and meetings. Even when others are speaking, many of us are not truly silent on the inside, as we work out what we are going to say next. Embracing silence in our personal lives will also help us to really listen to others when they are speaking. Those with whom you communicate will feel far more valued, as they will know you are truly listening; and when you next have something to say, your silence will be helpful as you will have truly listened to what has been said. In fact, those who speak less in meetings are considered wiser by the others in the room, which means that silence not only means that you will listen better, but you will also be listened to more intently when you speak. As Plato is reputed to have said, 'Wise men speak because they have something to say; fools because they have to say something.'

There is power too in collective silence; for example, the silence we use at a national level to remember those who have fallen in wars. These memorial silences used to be two minutes long, but now seem to have reduced to one minute, and are accompanied by clapping in some cases. It's almost as if silence is too difficult for us in these days of minuscule attention spans. Let's go back to longer silences, shall we? Maybe I should start a petition? I remember when on a spiritual walk in India, though there were thirteen of us, we sometimes spent an hour walking in 'noble silence' and there was a power to it that I hadn't ever experienced before. With even larger groups, there is potentially more power.

One year on from the appalling fire in Grenfell Tower in London, which unnecessarily killed 72 people, there was a silent walk to remember the victims and to call for justice. Here are the words of Lisa Cumming who was on that walk:

> I've gathered together in communities after tragic, violent events – riots, floods – before, but I've never experienced the strength, compassion and power of the multitude who came together one year on from the Grenfell Tower fire... Someone was playing piano. Some gentle hushing told us that it was time for the silent walk to start. Old, young, survivors and supporters had gathered in huge numbers. As we waited, a young man in a high-vis jacket asked people to hold the silence, just a couple of polite reminders was all it took. And

the silence held... I've been learning lots about the collective power of silence since starting to work for Quakers. And the silence for Grenfell was held by the most incredible community supporting one another in grief, while searching for the three words that kept echoing in the signs people carried – love, truth, justice.

I usually post a two-minute video each week on social media talking about some aspect of good leadership, but recently as I upload the videos I feel slightly conflicted, as I am aware I am putting more words out into the world when there are probably too many there already. Maybe one week I should act like John Cage and post a two-minute video of me sitting in silence. Maybe it would have more impact? Individual silence is powerful, as is collective silence. Let's incorporate more silence into our own noisy world which will make us better leaders.

Actions

Learn to live with silence as part of your life:

» Right now, set a stopwatch alarm for five minutes, and be silent. When your mind wanders, bring it back and focus on your breathing, which will help. Enjoy the silence.

» Today, find some other time to be in silence. If you come from a busy home to a busy work situation (or vice versa), it's all the more necessary to find a place where you can be quiet. Make this a habit and try to do it daily.

» In meetings or conversations today, actively listen in silence for longer than you would normally. Learn not to be afraid of silence in conversations. Fewer words often equals wiser words.

DAY 27 » **Resilient**

Dictionary definition:

> 'Recovering easily and quickly from shock, illness, hardship, etc.:
> irrepressible.'
>> *Collins English Dictionary*

Quotes:

> 'Resilience is very different than being numb. Resilience means you
> experience, you feel, you fail, you hurt. You fall. But, you keep going.'
>> *Yasmin Mogahed, American psychologist*

> 'Do not judge me by my success, judge me by how many times I fell
> down and got back up again.'
>> *Nelson Mandela, South African anti-apartheid revolutionary*

> 'Life doesn't get easier or more forgiving, we get stronger and more
> resilient.'
>> *Steve Maraboli, American author and leadership coach*

> 'The human capacity for burden is like bamboo – far more flexible
> than you'd ever believe at first glance.'
>> *Jodi Picoult, American novelist*

Insights

If there was an adjective for 'bouncebackability', I might have used that as today's chapter heading. In fact, I looked up 'bouncebackability' and found that this word was first used by Iain Dowie about his football team, Crystal Palace, to describe their ability to bounce back after a string of terrible results. It certainly describes the exact same characteristics I am writing about here, which are essential for a good leader or indeed anyone wanting to make a positive difference in the world. Talk to any successful person and 99 per cent of the time, they will admit to having failed on more than one occasion and to having been repeatedly knocked back when attempting to fulfil their purpose or mission. Many would agree that the key to being a great leader (rather than just an OK one) is the ability to bounce back from defeat or abject failure. We are all bound to have tough times in our lives, and if we are leading others, it is clearly important that we don't drag them down with us.

So, how do we develop resilience? I am convinced there are no magic wands or shortcuts here. It is simply about going through hard times, learning through them and becoming stronger for next time. As an old friend of mine used to say, 'The school colours of the University of Life are black and blue.' Allow me to relate one of my own experiences. In 2014, we had a successful business and were about to install a new warehouse management system, which would eliminate paperwork from our warehouse. First, a week before the 'go live' date, two key members of the team had to be removed from the company for stealing stock. Second, and more significantly, the IT installation went very badly due to our data not having enough integrity, leading to a first week from hell with the new system. This was followed four days later by a flood, which wiped out around 20 metres of a warehouse aisle full of stock. Two days after that, I received a phone call advising me that my operations director, the leader of the warehouse operation, had been rushed into hospital with a suspected heart attack, and we wouldn't be seeing him until many weeks later. The company I had spent 15 years building up was suddenly on its knees. Customers and suppliers were both receiving appalling service and several members of my team of around 45 people decided to leave the company due to the pressure of delivering terrible service for two months.

At this point I was at rock bottom, the second time in five years, the previous time being after my first marriage broke up. To try and recover the company my default operating mode was to run around like a headless chicken, which never has achieved very much. In my time at home, largely during the middle of the night, I started to face the probability that this would be the end of my company. As I started to come to terms with this, I realised that much of my identity was tied up in my own success, i.e. what I did, rather than being secure and confident in who I was. On talking to many other leaders about this since, I've discovered this is a very common problem, and it is essential to find our true identity in who we are rather than what we do in order to develop resilience.

Back in 2014 over a few vital weeks, I mentally let go of all the success and trappings of success and started to imagine life without the company. I eventually came to a position of being happy to accept whatever happened. Of course, I still wanted everything to work out – especially for all those who worked for me – but I was no longer attached to a positive outcome. As it turned out, we managed to turn the business around and I would now say that it marked a distinct turning point towards building the much more purpose-driven, happier business we have today. I am absolutely convinced that lack of attachment is key to resilience. It's not that you don't feel the pain and hardship, but you know that you as a person will come out the other side much stronger whatever happens. It's a hard lesson to learn but dealing with adversity becomes easier the more times you go through it.

Jump forward five years and we changed the company logistics by moving warehouse, which was going to reduce our carbon impact by 46 per cent – and everything went very wrong again. This time, though, due to the resilience built up five years previously, which over half the management team had experienced too, there was a completely different sense of determination and a positive atmosphere that we were going to get through it. The pain and exasperation were still there, but everyone knew we had made the decision for the right reasons and we were united around that purpose.

In his book *Bounce*, Matthew Syed uses the term 'grit'. He says that grit or resilience is a powerful predictor of success in everything from maths to music. Those who screw up, make loads of mistakes but keep going are the ones who are more likely to succeed. Syed says that the neurological architecture of the brain changes if people stick at things. So, resilience isn't a genetic trait but one that comes from practice, experience and failure. I love the word grit as it reminds me of falling over as a kid on a rough surface and scraping all the skin off my knees on a rough, gritty surface. It hurts like hell, but usually heals perfectly.

In 1888, Nietzsche wrote, *'Aus der Kriegsschule des Lebens – Was mich nicht umbringt, macht mich starker'*, which can be translated as 'Out of life's school of war – what doesn't kill me makes me stronger.' This statement appears in a book of aphorisms and he gives no further explanation of it, which is interesting, as everyone knows intuitively and through their own experience that it is absolutely true. We also know from the amazing experiences of several beautiful people we may have met, full of love, who have been through the most appalling disasters, tragedies and wars. We know through meeting paraplegics who, to our shame, are fuller of gratitude than we are. And we know we are made stronger through our own bad experiences, looking back at our own lives and seeing how we have grown from the young, rather stupid person we once were to who we are today.

Being a good leader is about coming through these difficult times with a smile on our face, renewed determination and grit in our heart, knowing that we are better people who are more able to make a positive difference in other people's lives through the development of our own character. The resilient are those leaders that others will want to follow.

Actions

Resilience takes a lifetime to develop, but what we can do today is:

- » Look back at a difficult time in your life – choose the first event that comes to mind – and reflect on how that changed you as a person. Be thankful for that time. Knowing that strength of character is built in challenging times will sustain you in the future.

- » Are you going through difficulties at present? If so, in this moment consciously separate what you do from who you are. You are more important than the success of a business or a relationship. You will get through it.

- » If you are going through a difficult time today, find a shoulder to cry on. Alternatively, perhaps you could be that shoulder for someone else? Make a phone call or send a message today to someone who may need your support in their time of difficulty.

DAY 28 » **Collaborative**

Dictionary definition:

'Involving two or more people working together for a special purpose.'
Cambridge English Dictionary

Quotes:

'In the long history of humankind (and animal kind, too) those who learned to collaborate and improvise most effectively have prevailed.'
Charles Darwin, English naturalist and biologist

'Collaboration always wins over competition... and is more fun, too.'
Silvio Micali, Italian computer scientist

'Alone we can do so little; together we can do so much.'
Helen Keller, American author and political activist

'Collaboration has no hierarchy. The sun collaborates with soil to bring flowers on the earth.'
Amit Ray, Indian author and spiritual master

Insights

As mentioned, owing to the past imbalance of leadership, a lot of what comes into our heads when we imagine 'leadership' are typically masculine characteristics; so we must emphasise the feminine qualities to restore the balance and transition into a more rounded leadership for the 21st century. Being collaborative is certainly one of these qualities; women are innately better at it than most men. For many men, in business and other areas, it has often been all about winning and defeating our competitors. When Donald Trump shouted, 'Make America great again!' he was doubtlessly thinking that other countries must lose out. Yet while it is easy to see who wins a football or tennis match, business and life aren't all about winning. Do you arrive at the end of your working life and say you've won? No! Do we come to the end of our financial year and say we won? Not really. We can say that we were above our budgetary plan and hit our targets, but as for winning and losing – probably not. Many have concluded that the financial crisis of 2008 only happened because there were large numbers of competitive men in dealing rooms who didn't share information and collaborate like women would have done.

Simon Sinek talks about moving away from this winning and losing mindset in his book *The Infinite Game*, saying that many people (mostly men) have played infinite games, such as those of business and life, in a finite way – resulting in much frustration, unhappiness and ultimately damage to both people and the planet. This is one of the main reasons collaboration is in short supply in some environments. Take mergers, for example, which very rarely involve an actual merger but are more likely to be a takeover by one company of the other, often implemented to make one executive look bigger than another and look like he (and, yes, usually a man again) has won. However, up to an astonishing 83 per cent of mergers fail according to KPMG. In a situation when collaboration is needed more than anything, most of those types of leaders probably aren't capable of it, due to their finite approach.

Competition rather than collaboration is a central tenet of the capitalist economy, with 'let the market decide' being one of its favourite mantras. It is now widely acknowledged that many of capitalism's non-negotiables are up for debate, and moving from a competitive economy to a collaborative one must surely be high up the list. Mathematicians have always argued in favour of collaboration being a better strategy than competition, because it yields better outcomes. The brilliant Eve Poole puts this far better than I could in her blog post '7

Deadly Sins – capitalism's flat-earth problem and what to do about it', written in 2014:

> Those who treat transactions as battles to be won or lost sooner or later come a cropper, as their brand tarnishes and the market votes them out. On the other hand, co-operation and the sharing of information increases the size of the pie, instead of restricting the debate to arguments about how best to cut it up. And competition isn't just mathematically questionable, it's sexist, too. While male fight-or-flight physiology favours competition, particularly in challenging environments, it ignores the role that female physiology has to play. Research conducted on female subjects suggests quite a different physiological response, one that has been dubbed 'tend and befriend'. So being hooked on competition may actually be compounding a tendency towards sub-optimal outcomes, reinforced through the norms of a traditionally masculine business environment.

In my own small world of speciality food and drink wholesale, it so happens that the vast majority of other wholesalers are run by exclusively male leadership teams (unlike us), and – from what I have heard – there appears to be a tendency among them to obsess about what our company is doing, rather than focus on what they themselves are doing. Within our company we have banned ourselves from using the word 'competitor' to describe them, preferring the term 'other wholesalers' if we must talk about them. In fact, I heard today that one of them might be about to go out of business. This made me feel sad rather than happy, because it is bad for the industry, as we all effectively have the same purpose of encouraging consumers to eat better; and all wholesalers reduce carbon within the supply chain. In many industries, however, notably within the digital economy, collaboration is the normal way to behave, but even there, it only happens to a degree and then that old competitiveness kicks in. So, what is it that makes us a truly collaborative leader at heart, rather than just a tactically collaborative one?

One of our main troubles in the West is that we think our highly individualistic way of living is normal, when historically humans have been far more community-orientated and collaborative than we are now used to. Set in the context of the history of humanity, it is highly abnormal to shut ourselves away in isolated houses, behind closed gates, after we drive home of an evening. In this broader historical context, it is also unusual to accumulate vehicles and possessions without a thought of sharing them with others. It would be bizarre in many cultures to respect people more because they lived in a larger house or drove a more expensive car than us. In fact, in some cultures, such as those of Ecuador or Indonesia, individuals who have excess possessions but who do not share them with the community would be viewed as strange and perhaps in need of psychological help. Of course, much of our own society's hyper-materialism comes from people's insecurities and the need for them to feel better about themselves by impressing others.

Truly collaborative people will not mind sharing information and possessions if it helps the community or workplace as a whole. They will be pleased when others receive praise for something that they know was largely due to their combined efforts. They will know that anything they achieve is only because they are standing on the shoulders of giants who have gone before them, or who may even still be there helping them in the background. Perhaps the most important factor in being collaborative is to know our own weaknesses. When people ask what I am particularly good at within business, I tend to reply that I am only really good at one thing and that is finding people much better than me to look after all the different areas of the business in a spirit of collaboration. There is good statistical evidence from start-ups that businesses started with co-founders (two or more) have a much greater chance of success than those started by one person, and even more so if the co-founders have complementary skills. This was the case at the start of Cotswold Fayre, when I worked with a co-founder who had the exact opposite skills to me, and while the partnership only lasted two years before an amicable parting, the pattern of collaboration was set for the rest of the life of the business. I was then, and am now even more so, very aware of my weaknesses – and this has driven me to collaboration more than anything else. There really is only room for collaborative leaders as we face the challenges of this third decade of the 21st century.

Actions

Let's start by making today a day of collaboration:

» How aware are you of your weaknesses? Reflect for a short time and then journal a list of your weaknesses. For each one, ask yourself whether someone in your business or organisation has the skills to complement and offset it.

» How important is it for you to win? Are you happy letting others enjoy the rewards of what you might have done? If not, why not?

» Today, walk around (mentally or in reality) the different parts of your organisation or business and be open to ideas where collaboration could increase. Take a notebook with you.

DAY 29 » **Interdependent**

Dictionary definition:

'Interdependence is the condition of a group of people or things that all depend on each other.'
Collins English Dictionary

Quotes:

'The whole idea of compassion is based on a keen awareness of the interdependence of all these living beings, which are all part of one another, and all involved in one another.'
Thomas Merton, American Trappist monk

'Interdependence is a fundamental law of nature. Even tiny insects survive by mutual cooperation based on innate recognition of their interconnectedness. It is because our own human existence is so dependent on the help of others that our need for love lies at the very foundation of our existence. Therefore we need a genuine sense of responsibility and a sincere concern for the welfare of others.'
Dalai Lama, Tibetan spiritual leader

'No individual or nation can stand out boasting of being independent. We are interdependent.'
Martin Luther King, Jr. American civil rights activist

'The fundamental law of human beings is interdependence. A person is a person through other persons.'
Desmond Tutu, South African cleric and theologian

Insights

The word 'interdependent' is not often used of people, but here I am talking about being aware of our interdependence or, better still, learning to be the opposite of individualistic. I was going to use the words 'community-orientated', which is also valid on a local scale, but I wanted to find a word that conveyed the breadth of our reliance on the rest of the world in all aspects: vegetable, mineral and animal. There are synergies in today's thoughts with those we will look at in the 'Connected' chapter (Day 32), but today I am focusing on an awareness of our interdependence as an antidote to the rampant individualism that is now endemic in our Western culture. Losing that ingrained cultural independence and individuality and moving towards interdependence are not only paramount to our happiness and success, but also essential for our planet itself.

My brother lives near Muir Woods in Marin County, California, and I have twice been to see the coastal redwoods while visiting him. I remember standing for nearly an hour and looking up into the canopy, absolutely astonished at the sheer height of those amazing trees. Any photos you have seen simply do not do them justice. Some of these trees are 300 feet tall and over 2,500 years old, so you would expect them to have the most amazing root system that reaches down hundreds of feet into the earth to draw water from it and provide them with enough stability. I later found out that the root systems of these giants of the plant world are actually very shallow indeed, but all the roots are intertwined. They are completely locked to each other and despite storms and strong winds very rarely fall down because the trees support and protect each other. This is a lovely symbol of interdependence.

Many of us have been indoctrinated through our education and upbringing to think of ourselves as isolated individuals, to maximise our income whatever the impact to others, and to buy products as cheaply as possible whatever the impact to the much poorer country where the product is made. We have been educated, particularly in a business setting, to win at all costs; we cannot possibly lose. As business leaders, we can easily tell ourselves stories that we deserve to win as an individual and say to ourselves, 'We have worked twelve-hour days for this for years; so what if others in the world are in poverty – we deserve our success.' There is nothing wrong with enjoying some of the luxuries of life, but if other people in our company, our community or within our supply chains are suffering as a result, we have a massive problem. As Martin Luther King said, 'As long as there is poverty in the world I can never be rich, even if I have a billion dollars.'

Our lack of understanding of our interdependence with the planet itself is now taking a terrible toll, and it remains uncertain whether we can reverse this manmade decline. For years, we have chewed through planetary resources at an ever-increasing rate – to win the race to where exactly? Now, as the planet's infrastructure is falling apart due to climate change, we won't carry on 'winning' for too much longer, as we will all be impacted by the damage that we, our parents and grandparents have done. I have seen some commentators suggest that the coronavirus pandemic of 2020 was nature's way of calling us to order. 'This irresponsible churning through my resources must stop!' Mother Nature seemingly cries out. If you think that takes things too far, the fact that what happened on a 'wet market' in Wuhan could have an impact on the whole world within a month or two, must make us see – if nothing else – the absolute interdependence of nearly 8 billion people. We are not isolated families entitled to better ourselves without thinking of others; neither do we have the right to think of ourselves as merely individual communities, cities or nations. In the 21st century, the whole of humanity is interconnected and interdependent. The American Dream has potentially turned into a nightmare in Vietnam, India and Tanzania.

So, how do we become more 'interdependent' as people and leaders? The transition comes down to our choices. As individual consumers, we simply can't let money be the only factor in our purchasing decisions any longer. The cheapest products are often those that have the most detrimental impact on others around the world and on the planet itself. Within the food and drink sector, most buying decisions are made purely based on price, without any regard for the social or planetary cost. Attitudes are changing, albeit slowly, but we, as consumers, can help speed the change by changing some of our own individual purchasing habits. Another necessary change is to ensure that everyone can make these choices by reducing inequality, as far too many people are still paid lower than the real living wage – and to think that this inequality doesn't impact the whole of society is extremely naive. Some of the required changes need to be led by governmental policy to force employers to change their individualistic un-interdependent behaviour. On the planetary side, this is certainly true. In the UK, we have made some progress, but it is far too slow. Our growth in sustainability is stunted, because there aren't nearly enough subsidies around to transform people's individualistic behaviour. For example, decent-sized electric cars with reasonable range are still beyond the budget of most working families. That the government could suddenly pay 80 per cent of the wages of around 30 per cent of the UK population during the Covid-19 crisis in 2020 shows what can be done when governments do put their minds to it. The same urgency needs to be shown towards the climate emergency, yet the UK and many other governments are still subsidising the fossil fuel industry.

Since this book is primarily designed to help with personal growth, let's bring ourselves back to that focus. As individuals, we can sometimes think the task is too big for us, but it is important not to let perfection get in the way of progress. We can all do something today to demonstrate our interdependence, something slightly more significant next week, and something even more transformational next year. In fact, as leaders we must change the way we live because others are watching our choices. As our understanding increases and if companies have to provide evidence of care for people and planet to consumers, in ten years' time we may have shifted the needle from being a predominantly individualistic society to being a truly interdependent one. As people and leaders, we may, as Desmond Tutu said, discover our real personhood: 'The fundamental law of human beings is interdependence. A person is a person through other persons.' We simply cannot afford to delay understanding our interdependence at a profound level, for the lives of others depend on it.

Actions

Let's grow into our interdependence:

» Imagine for a few minutes those shallow, intertwined roots of the redwoods. Think of some your possessions and daily activities – and imagine how and with whom the roots of these are intertwined.

» Write down a few thoughts on how your own behaviour and lifestyle is individualistic, the opposite of interdependent. What can you do to change personally over the next year? What can you do to change your business or organisation?

» Today, change a buying decision or activity to one that will benefit others or the planet.

DAY 30 » **Purposeful**

Dictionary definition:

'Determined to achieve an aim.'
Macmillan Dictionary

Quotes:

'The purpose of life is to obey the hidden command which ensures harmony among all and creates an ever better world. We are not created only to enjoy the world, we are created in order to evolve the cosmos.'
Maria Montessori, Italian physician and educator

'The important thing is that men should have a purpose in life. It should be something useful, something good.'
Dalai Lama, Tibetan spiritual leader

'There is one quality that one must possess to win, and that is definiteness of purpose, the knowledge of what one wants, and a burning desire to possess it.'
Napoleon Hill, American self-help author

'It's easy to confuse a lot of activity with a purposeful life. Do what lasts; let the rest fall away.'
Bob Goff, American lawyer and speaker

Insights

I am sure many of us are familiar with Simon Sinek's *Start with Why*, still one of the most viewed Ted Talks of all time. Sinek was primarily talking about the purpose of a company in that talk, the DNA behind what the company does or makes and what they are achieving in the world. Many companies now embrace purpose or their 'why' and have a clear expression of their purpose on their website and company literature; in fact, company purpose statements have almost become the norm. What I have discovered, though, is that there are far fewer individuals who are clear on their personal 'why' or their individual purpose in life. Some people bumble around, flitting from one job to another or one project to another without having a grander reason for what they do in life. Others have clear definition of their different roles but haven't ever clearly defined their purpose. I was one of the bumblers: I had a vague notion of wanting to make the world better in some way, but hadn't really distilled that down and articulated it properly.

What's remarkable is that every one of the nearly 8 billion people on earth is different. Not only do we all look different (remarkable in itself) but everyone has had individual experiences in life, meaning that what excites them, drives them and makes them sad will be different than for the next person. Let's think about that a little more deeply for a moment. You as an individual are different to the other 7.8 billion people on earth. Your experiences mean that you are unique and have different passions, skills and purpose to anyone else on earth. That may seem like a trite thing to say, but when you let the information sink in, it can be amazing to think that because of who you are, you too can achieve something unique on earth, something no one else could do in quite the same way. This sounds slightly simplistic when written down, but when we realise the significance of our individuality in this respect, it can spur us on to discover our purpose, knowing that we are here to achieve something unique. And the marvellous thing is that even the painful experiences that have moulded you as a person are part of the process that makes you unique. The trauma and sadness we may have experienced really can be turned to good; in fact, those who have experienced great difficulties often go on to achieve great things.

So, are you clear on your purpose? Do you know why you are here on this planet? If not, or even if you know part of the answer, then discovering your purpose, I believe, is important to having a fulfilled and happy life. There are various ways of helping us discover our purpose. One is the thought experiment of imagining yourself at the end of your life, maybe even your own funeral (which sounds a little morbid, I know, but bear with me), looking back on your life and what you have achieved, and imagining what you would like others to be saying about you. What do you want them to be saying about your life? Another method is to jump backwards into your childhood via a guided meditation. Remembering yourself at the age of 6 and then 12 and then 18 and asking yourself what you were passionate about at those ages and what upset you. Sometimes the heart of who we are can be crowded out by 'adult' activities and we can end up going through the motions in life, forgetting to focus on what we dreamed about when younger. The third method is to ask your friends, but not your immediate family, what they think your purpose in life is. Ask them what is different about you and where you make a difference. Often, they will give you a similar answer, which should help. Finally, ask yourself what you are good at and what you love: hopefully there is some crossover between the two. Often our gifts and skills are an important part of our purpose.

As I've already mentioned, I had a woolly sense of my purpose for much of my adulthood, and, as a result, my life has been a little like a sine curve, wandering above and below the line of my purpose. Earlier in this book, I described going on a 'holy walk' in India, during which a group of twelve men, half of whom were Indian and half non-Indian, walked along the banks of a river for eight days and slept on ashram (temple) floors at night. It was a truly remarkable experience that was modelled on a shortened version of the eight-week passage of a boy to a man in Hinduism, with each day taking the theme of one of those weeks. The first couple of days were about throwing off everything that holds us back; then there was a journeying phase in the middle; and we concluded with a couple of days on the theme of arriving, which, with the internal work that had previously happened, helped us gain clarity on our purpose. I was encouraged to write a purpose statement, which was honed over several days during and after the walk. It may well evolve in the future, but here it is as it currently stands:

> I open the hearts of leaders to bring love and compassion into both the business and political arenas, which will help reverse injustice and create a fairer and more sustainable world. Through my business activities and by my speaking and writing I will provoke and inspire lasting change.

I have found it very helpful to check in on this statement every so often, to make sure that I am maintaining my purpose. More importantly, it helps me say no to people who ask me to do events or activities that are not aligned with my purpose. For much of my life as a leader, I have been a 'doing' leader, rushing around in a life full of frenetic yet unfocused activity. Being clearer on my purpose has helped me do less but be more effective in what I do. That's what Bob Goff, the American author and speaker, is talking about when he says, 'Do what lasts; let the rest fall away.'

Passion and purpose are closely linked; hence a strong sense of motivation comes with being purposeful. Those with clear purpose do everything consistent with that purpose. Setbacks are bound to come, but once we find our purpose, not only will resilience increase but we will become more careful and selective about our daily actions.

Actions

Are you clear on your purpose?

» Do you have a purpose statement? Could you make a start on one today? If you don't know where to begin, reread the paragraph above – about the four ways of discovering your purpose – and make some notes.

» Whether you think you know your purpose in life or not, ask people today what they think your purpose is. It will be interesting to hear their answers!

» Are you doing any core activities this week that are not aligned with your purpose? Think about what they may be and start saying 'no'. Here I am talking about activities other than the mundane tasks like shopping and cleaning that we all have to do – although it is possible to find purpose in those too!

DAY 31 » **Loyal**

Dictionary definition:

'Firm and not changing in your friendship with or support for a person or an organization, or in your belief in your principles.'

Cambridge English Dictionary

Quotes:

'Outside of love, no two things are more valued in another person than trust and loyalty.'
Zig Ziglar, American author and salesman

'We are not here to be successful, we are here to be faithful.'
Mother Teresa, Albanian-Indian missionary

'Base yourself in loyalty and trust. Don't be a companion with those who are not your moral equal. When you make a mistake, don't hesitate to correct it.'
Confucius, Chinese philosopher

'Lack of loyalty is one of the major causes of failure in every walk of life.'
Napoleon Hill, American self-help author

Insights

Loyalty and faithfulness seem to be dying characteristics these days, with short-termism seemingly more in vogue both in personal relationships, supplier–customer relationships and employer–employee relationships. Now, there is a positive side to people being free to move on to better positions, but I would like to encourage some good old-fashioned loyalty while at the same time not staying in stale business relationships.

I've mentioned previously a time when Cotswold Fayre came close to going out of business completely. Due to a botched IT installation, customers were receiving around 50 per cent of their orders and sometimes not receiving them at all. Customer complaints were raining into our telesales office and the company was in a terrible place. In the middle of this carnage, one of our customers, who was a well-respected consultant in the food retail world, ran an industry workshop where the subject of our company's poor service came up. By this point, customers were moaning about us and some had stopped dealing with us altogether; but this wise, loyal customer, who was leading the workshop, told them that all businesses go through growing pains and these often occur around the time of IT implementations. She said that they should stick with us as loyal customers, as we had given good service in the past and would do so again soon. She was right.

In the short term, it would have been easier for customers to walk away from us at that point and go elsewhere, but loyalty is repaid. Of course, once our issues were sorted, we were particularly careful to give exceptional service to all those who had stuck with us and they enjoyed even better service than before. In fact, the customer who gave the seminar was also involved in a collaborative recruitment process to appoint our next salesperson in her area: she took part in the interview to choose her own account manager. In customer–supplier terms, if you are forced to make a choice between two, are you going to go the second mile for a customer who has been with you for ten years or for one who signed up the previous month?

It is virtually built into our psyche that the grass is always greener on the other side, yet it often isn't. Social media has increased opportunities for unfaithfulness and disloyalty like nothing has before. Stories of people reconnecting with old flames from school or university and breaking up their marriage are commonplace, and the ability to contact others easily in ways that were very difficult only a generation ago is a high contributing factor. In romantic relationships, it is easy to think that you would be happier in that potential new relationship, or the sex would be better if you ditched your current partner and went off with that guy who just contacted you out of the blue. In the short term, you may be right – there is a thrill involved in a new relationship – but the immediate high tends not to last very long and the cycle tends to be repeated with those who don't have loyalty as part of their character.

I have talked elsewhere about learning to let our heart or emotions become more involved in our decision making, but in terms of loyalty and faithfulness there is most definitely a case for putting our emotions into the background. Sticking to the prefrontal cortex, rational, decision-making part of our brain, and setting an intention and staying with it are the stuff of loyalty. As the leader of a company, you simply can't just jump ship when the going gets tough and it is good to foster this attitude both in those you lead and in your personal relationships. Sometimes we seem programmed to see the faults of others, rather than the positive attributes. Disciplining our minds to look for the positives in others will help make us more loyal and faithful people and leaders.

Others are both watching and helping us with our loyalty. Aside from the legal niceties, there is nothing magic about the state of people who are married and those who are not. In olden days, and in some cultures today, sexual union was the difference that sealed the change in the relationship status. Today, though, if there is any magic in the wedding ceremony it is in the fact that you make a promise in front of many witnesses, who are then meant to help you stay loyal and faithful to those promises. Good friends or witnesses are there to help you come through difficulties and honour the commitment. Likewise, it is important for leaders to have others they can talk to in challenging times that may lead to disloyalty.

There are, of course, many people involved in destructive and abusive relationships both personally and unfortunately within companies. Sometimes, partners and employers simply need to cut their ties and leave in a way that damages themselves and others as little as possible. Only yesterday, I heard from someone who is working for a company that is treating them appallingly, and despite complaints being made, this has continued. I advised them to leave as soon as possible for their own wellbeing. It is, of course, the same in personal relationships: abuse must be always be walked away from and those hurting ones will often need friends to help them do that. As Confucius said, 'Base yourself in loyalty and trust. Don't be a companion with those who are not your moral equal.'

If you are an employer, there are great reasons to stay faithful and loyal to your people, and to forgive mistakes when they happen, even covering for these where necessary. The 'hire and fire' culture never built a great company, but the faithful and loyal character of leaders will encourage the same traits in their colleagues. As leaders, one of the costliest parts of running a business is recruiting and training people. Reducing churn and increasing loyalty and faithfulness amongst those who work for us comes through creating a nurturing atmosphere and defending them with fierce loyalty when customers or suppliers are attacking them. Even if our people have made mistakes, we can learn from those professional football managers who never hang their players out to dry in the media but will defend them to the hilt. Any words that need to be said are said in private.

While I was researching the quotes for this section, most of the 'faithful' quotes were to do with dogs and most of the 'unfaithful' quotes were about men. How sad is that? In this instance, it pays to go to the dogs and show that same degree of loyalty and faithfulness to others. Remember the powerful words of Zig Ziglar: 'Outside of love, no two things are more valued in another person than trust and loyalty.'

Actions

Let's think about our own loyalty and faithfulness today:

- » Most of us have been disloyal or unfaithful on occasions. Rather than brooding over it, quietly think for a few moments about what prompted that behaviour.
- » At work, as a colleague or leader, how loyal are you to others? How good are you at seeing the positives? How good are you at giving others a second chance?
- » What could you do to increase the loyalty of the people within your business to each other? Is there anything that needs changing in your work culture?

DAY 32 » **Connected**

Dictionary definition:

'Joined or linked together.'
Collins English Dictionary

Quotes:

'Study how water flows in a valley stream, smoothly and freely between the rocks. Also learn from holy books and wise people. Everything – even mountains, rivers, plants and trees – should be your teacher.'
Morihei Ueshiba, Japanese martial artist

'Look deep into nature, and then you will understand everything better.'
Albert Einstein, German theoretical physicist

'Only through our connectedness to others can we really know and enhance the self. And only through working on the self can we begin to enhance our connectedness to others.'
Harriet Goldhor Lerner, American psychologist

'Making a strong connection with people is never easy. It is even more difficult to connect with people who are very different from you.'
Abhishek Ratna, American author and coach

Insights

The trouble with our neoliberalist Western culture is that it has given too much importance to the cult of the individual and relegated our connection to both nature and other people to a secondary position. Margaret Thatcher's oft-quoted words from an interview in *Woman's Own* in 1987 summarised the spirit of the age: 'And, you know, there's no such thing as society. There are individual men and women and there are families. And no government can do anything except through people, and people must look after themselves first.' There has been a level of progression in the 21st century but there is much for us to re-learn in terms of being connected to the rest of our world, in terms of being connected to both the people and nature itself. Our ancestors knew what it was to be connected; we must understand what this means in the 21st century.

Scientific progression has often been blamed for the loss of wonder in nature so I love the fact that Albert Einstein, probably the most eminent scientist of all, still seems to have had a sense of wonder about the natural world, suggesting that we can gain greater understanding through looking deeply into nature. We can learn a huge amount in this area from the developing world about where we have gone wrong in the West. In the West, we have typically regarded all the other living organisms in the world as being below humans in a 'we shall have dominion over them' sense. Children in the West are even taught that *Homo sapiens* is the boss over the whole living world, with other mammals ranking directly below them and all other living organisms below mammals in turn. To understand our connectedness, it is much better to imagine all life existing in a circle, with no life form ranking above another: humans not as boss but working in partnership and symbiosis with the rest of life.

Many of those living from the land – particularly in highly agricultural economies – see the world in a more wholesome way. They do not see the earth as a resource from which we can carry on taking until it can give no more, but they recognise a connectivity with nature and collaborate with the other living creatures within the world. I heard once of some South American Indians who loved to catch salmon at the time of year when the fish swim from the sea up the rivers to breed. However, every year they would let the salmon swim upstream for four days before they started to fish, ensuring many fish were able to breed and sustain the population for the following season. Their connection with nature helps them cooperate with it, rather than ruthlessly exploiting it – which is Western man's tendency.

I have already talked about going for walks in the countryside, and while exercise and being alone are important, for me, a large part of walking in nature is about connecting with the world and the life within it. To be in awe of creation, and to be amazed by the intricacies and detail within it, do us the power of good. I believe that creation can speak to us; we can find answers to some of our dilemmas within it and we can sometimes understand the way forward more clearly through looking and listening to nature. A couple of years ago, I started to sense a calling to a change of direction, with the aim of passing on to others some of the insights I have gained over the years in life and business. Some of my awareness of this potential new direction came through observing the signs in nature as I walked around thinking. While on a retreat last year, I was encouraged to speak directly to nature again, and it's not just a one-way communication. We talk to our pets, so why not talk to other animals and trees? Maybe I should stop here, before you think I've lost the plot, but there's a wonderful sense of joy of being connected to the living world, as St Francis of Assisi discovered!

For this day, I have deliberately chosen two quotes about connecting with nature and two about connecting with people. Learning to be connected is about both types of connection and both are, of course, equally important in ridding us of the cult of the individual. During the course of my life and work, I have been fortunate to have had to learn to connect with people from all sorts of different backgrounds from within the UK and beyond; from depressed, out-of-work single parents in the inner city to public school boys at Oxford University, and from tribal farmers in Africa to landowner-farmers in the UK. I agree with Abhishek Ratna: it is more difficult to connect to those different from us, but when we learn to do this, we can learn far more from them than people who are like us. Those from other backgrounds can challenge our narrow-minded thinking and help remove the blinkers from our rather restricted philosophical worldview.

Just as in our misguided view of man's dominance over nature, we Westerners have seen ourselves at the top of a pyramid, below which are people from less affluent, more agriculturally based societies. How wrong could we possibly be? We have huge amounts to learn from them about connectedness with others and nature. Urbanisation and industrialisation have broken the bonds between us in both aspects. It is time to reconnect and learn to get under the skin of others. To understand how others think, how they feel, their joys and their tribulations. Not only can we learn, but we will also grow in our love for others and in our love and understanding of ourselves. From Harriet Goldhor Lerner's insight, we learn that it is a process with a positive feedback loop: through connecting to others, we know ourselves and through knowing ourselves, we are in a better position to reach out to others. Developing ourselves as leaders, while in part is about spending time on our own and understanding ourselves, is just as much about reaching out and connecting with others. How well are you connected to both people and the planet?

Actions

Today, let's start learning to connect deeply with others and nature:

» Reflect for a few minutes on where you position yourself as a human within the web of the world. Do you think of humans as ranking above or intricately connected with all of nature? Picture all living beings in your mind: where do you sit?

» Go for a walk in the country, or in a park if you live in a city, and connect with some part of nature. It could be something as small as an insect or as large as a tree. Do what Einstein did and look deep into nature to try to understand everything a little better.

» Try to connect with someone you do not normally talk to. It could be that homeless girl on the street or the café-worker making your sandwich at lunchtime.

DAY 33 » **Peace-loving**

Dictionary definition:

'Peace-loving: Liking peace and trying to live and act in a way that will bring it.'
   Cambridge English Dictionary

'Peace: Freedom from war and violence, especially when people live and work together without disagreements.'
   Cambridge English Dictionary

Quotes:

'If we have no peace, it is because we have forgotten that we belong to each other.'
   Mother Teresa, Albanian-Indian missionary

'We look forward to the time when the Power of Love will replace the Love of Power. Then will our world know the blessings of peace.'
   William E. Gladstone, British statesman and politician

'It is not enough to say we must not wage war. It is necessary to love peace and sacrifice for it.'
   Martin Luther King, Jr., American civil rights activist

'Lord, make me an instrument of thy peace. Where there is hatred, let me sow love.'
   St Francis of Assisi, Italian friar, mystic and preacher

Insights

The choice of wording is important here. Here, I am not talking about inner peace (which I cover on Day 47, when we look at being calm), but about being a lover of peace and someone who is committed to non-violent or non-angry solutions to conflict. Of course, the two characteristics are connected; those leaders who are at peace within themselves are less likely to rush into a conflict, whereas business or political leaders with anger issues are more likely to employ bullying tactics with their competitors or, in politics, send their people to war. What I am talking about here is a commitment to non-violence, which will impact us on a day-to-day level and, if we are political leaders, help us resolve conflicts without war.

I am someone who came out of their teenage years quite angry and I am still learning the ways of peace on a personal level. I also maintain the right kind of anger against injustice, and politically I am committed to peace at all costs. I therefore find it difficult to relate to anyone who is comfortable going to work at a munition's factory, for example, knowing that the fruit of their day's work is to create a device that destroys fellow human beings. I also would say that if a small fraction of the money that is spent on armed forces were to be spent on conflict resolution endeavours, then the world would be a more peaceful place in which to live. After all, 22 countries in the world have no armed forces and seem to get on just fine, Costa Rica being one of the better known, despite being adjacent to a war-torn Nicaragua for many years in the 20th century. This is not a book on politics, but there are areas where our inner character impacts our outer actions and beliefs that mean it is sometimes difficult to stay out of the political arena. The need to win, largely a masculine trait, has fuelled many a war, and I do wonder whether if more women had led countries over the years, the number of wars would have decreased significantly. Many think the answer to this hypothetical question is almost certainly 'yes'.

Let's discuss, though, what a commitment to being peace-loving or nonviolent means for leaders like us. We have several amazing examples here. One is Desmond Tutu, who was instrumental in ending apartheid in South Africa and who was committed to finding a nonviolent solution throughout. At the peak of violence against Blacks and immediately after a particularly brutal massacre of Black people in Johannesburg, he said, 'Do not hate. Let us choose the peaceful way to freedom.' Before Tutu's era, Mahatma Gandhi developed his principles of nonviolent resistance in South Africa before he used them to great impact in his home country of India. It was also Gandhi that Martin Luther King Jr. looked to as an example to follow in his work as a more recent well-known practitioner of non-violence.

As I was preparing to write this chapter, the main headlines on yesterday evening's news described the racial tension in the USA. The reaction of the oppressed Black minority population has been exhibited by some in fighting with the oppressive police force and by others in looting shops, but one group simply filled an area of the city and knelt on one knee in silent protest. I would challenge anyone not to see the far greater power in nonviolent protest than violence from a minority, which will always be shut down by the more powerful majority.

If we are the kind of leaders that want justice for the two billion people in the world whose living standards fall short of the United Nation's Sustainable Development Goals in terms of poverty, sanitation, education and the like, we may have to resist those who stand in the way of equality. If you think you live in a country where that isn't necessary, don't forget that there are many things that have happened recently that we never thought possible – we are living in politically turbulent times. So, let's take a brief look at Martin Luther King's principles about resisting evil without resorting to violence and apply them to all levels of our lives.

King was passionate about winning the friendship and understanding of his opponents without humiliating them. How many of us do this in our daily lives; we are usually conditioned to think in terms of winning, which is not the peace-lover's way. King also said it is important to distinguish that it is the evil itself which should be resisted – not the person doing the evil acts, an important difference. He advocated that those resisting violence should be prepared to suffer as a consequence, as suffering can be redemptive and win over minds. King was keen to make it clear that peaceful protest was not just about desisting from violent acts, but that it was also important not to possess 'internal violence of the spirit'. In other words, hating your opponent is just as bad as shooting him. Finally, King encouraged people to have great faith in the future, as he believed that the universe is on the side of justice. That is a great thought to keep in mind when considering current inequalities, as we can look back through history and see the many wrongs that have been righted. Peace-loving is not about staying quiet and maintaining the status quo, because that is not going to result in a harmonious situation for those who aren't happy within the system.

So how can we become strong leaders who love peace and ensure any anger we feel doesn't end up being expressed in violent words or actions? We first have to distinguish between the different types of anger. One type of anger has more to do with our own ego, when we may feel put down by another, overlooked for promotion or insulted for who we are. We need to learn to push aside that kind of anger and perhaps work through our emotions in a quiet time of reflection, asking ourselves what exactly caused them to arise. If only our ego has been damaged then decide to try and stay calm; in time, we can learn to stop this type of anger rising and allow what others say and do to wash over us.

'Righteous' anger is linked to the pain we feel on behalf of others; for example, when someone has been wronged and we want to right that wrong. In these cases, the anger is a healthy emotion triggered by empathy and compassion for another, and it is good to keep the emotional feelings while engaging our thinking brain. After all, what good are violent words or actions going to do in such a situation? How many times has aggression sorted out a problem and resolved it? More often, it makes things worse. Those are the thoughts that our rational brains need to be 'saying' to the more emotional part of us – to enable us to keep our passion for justice but resist violence. This way the peace-lovers will win the day, and we know intuitively that these are the type of leaders that the world needs in the 21st century.

Actions

Let's discover more of what it means to be peace-loving today:

» When you feel rising anger, it is important to work out what is going on inside yourself. Is the anger caused by your ego or is it a healthier form of anger on behalf of others? Spend a while reflecting on what makes you angry and journal your thoughts now.

» Being a peace-lover is about viewing the person behind the wrong actions with compassion. Think of a time when you were angry with someone and try to reach out to them in your mind with love.

» To what extent is there any violent language towards customers, suppliers or, more likely, competitors in your workplace? If anything needs to change, why not start today?

DAY 34 » **Gentle**

Dictionary definition:

'Considerate or kindly in disposition; amiable and tender.'
Free Dictionary

Quotes:

'I choose gentleness... Nothing is won by force. I choose to be gentle. If I raise my voice, may it be only in praise. If I clench my fist, may it be only in prayer. If I make a demand, may it be only of myself.'
Max Lucado, American author and pastor

'Gentleness is the ability to bear reproaches and slights with moderation, and not to embark on revenge quickly, and not to be easily provoked to anger, but be free from bitterness and contentiousness, having tranquillity and stability in the spirit.'
Aristotle, Greek philosopher and polymath

'I place a high moral value on the way people behave. I find it repellent to have a lot, and to behave with anything other than courtesy in the old sense of the word – politeness of the heart, a gentleness of the spirit.'
Fran Lebowitz, American author and speaker

'Remember to be gentle with yourself and others. We are all children of chance and none can say why some fields will blossom while others lay brown beneath the August sun.'
Kent Nerburn, American author

Insights

One of Aesop's better-known fables is the story of 'The Wind and the Sun', who, one day, fell into an argument about who was the stronger. They decided to resolve their argument by a test; they would see which one of them could make a certain man, walking down the road, throw off his cape. The Wind tried first and blew and blew, but the harder and colder the Wind blew, the tighter the man wrapped his cape around him. The Wind gave up and it was the Sun's turn. The Sun began to smile and gently started to warm the man, very gradually at first, but the Sun shone brighter and brighter until the man grew so hot that sweat poured off his brow. The man soon became tired and sat down on a rock and removed his cape. The Sun's gentleness had triumphed over the Wind's show of strength.

There are similar stories throughout the world of how gentleness has achieved great things that power or strength has not. The Persian poet Shaykh al-Din Sa'di Shirazi put it beautifully: 'Use a sweet tongue, courtesy and gentleness and thou mayst manage to guide an elephant with a hair.' What a lovely image, moving an elephant with a hair! I realise how much I have to learn about gentleness, being prone myself to behaving like a bull in a china shop when events or people are not heading in what I feel is the right direction. I fear I behave more like the Wind in Aesop's story, huffing and puffing yet failing to blow the house down (to draw a parallel from another children's story). Gentleness can often achieve so much more and more quickly than shows of strength. As Max Lucado, poet and preacher, says, 'Nothing is won by force.' Let's really believe that: absolutely nothing is won by force.

The word 'gentleman' is not used in full very often these days, shortened instead to 'gents' or 'man'; however, from the beginning of its usage in the Middle Ages, the word had a sense of a nobleman whose behaviour conformed to the ideals of chivalry and Christianity. The term came to be used for any man of good breeding, courtesy and honour, showing a strict regard for other people's feelings. The phrase 'gentleman's agreement' carries with it a sense of decency, honour and courtesy that the phrase 'man's agreement' would not. I have mentioned in other places the need to balance femininity and masculinity within our management teams and this is not just a case of having at least an equal number of women as men on the teams, but also about men allowing the feminine sides of their characters to counterbalance their learned over-masculine behaviour. Gentleness is one characteristic that many men would do well to increase in their personalities.

I find the Kent Nerburn quote interesting, as I think it touches upon the root of some of our un-gentleness – the sense of not being gentle with ourselves, otherwise known as perfectionism. Often our culture and upbringing in the West drive us to perfectionism; this behaviour stems from our conditioned self and is something we need to 'un-condition' ourselves from by accepting ourselves more as we are. When we judge ourselves by impossible standards, this often leads to inner disappointment and sadness about our perceived failings. That is bad enough, but we sometimes turn those feelings outwards and project our perfectionist standards on to others – which removes our ability to be gentle with them. The real strength of a good relationship is when a measure of gentleness exists within them, whether they are work relationships or personal ones. Accepting others exactly as they are, and letting the warmth of our smile shine on them like the sun, will lift them up and we will start to see miracles within them. People are generally delicate beings and need more gentleness than we might imagine, even those who appear strong on the outside.

There is a plant on our patio with flowers that close at night-time and open when they feel the warmth of the sun around mid-morning. That is what gentleness can do within your family and workplace. Those that are closed with repressed creativity due to pain or misfortune, will open up when they are showed gentleness and kindness. In his autobiography, Mahatma Gandhi describes how he was almost inspired to become a Christian when reading about the exceedingly gentle way that Jesus dealt with people. He later said that it was Christians themselves that put him off, as they didn't behave like this at all. The way that Jesus is described as always lifting up the sick and needy with gentleness is incredibly inspiring, yet although being described as 'gentle Jesus, meek and mild' at Sunday school, it would be wrong to say that he avoided confrontation. There was the time when he made a whip to drive people out of the temple who were wrongly profiteering from religion, something that still goes on today. So, let us not think that to be gentle is always to avoid confrontation. It isn't, but it is probably about being involved in fewer confrontations and about those confrontations being more likely to have a just cause when we choose to engage.

One aspect of gentleness is about keeping silent when emotions such as anger or upset would try to tell us to do otherwise. Gentleness is about treading softly around people. I remember when we first brought our cat, Tom, back from the cat 'orphanage' and he really was a little scaredy-cat. Any sudden noise or movement would cause him to hide under the table. My wife and I had to earn the right to stroke him and even then he would only let us touch him in certain ways, and there were also times when he very clearly wanted to be left alone. We treated him with care and gentleness over a few months, and he completely changed. Now, five years later, he is one of the most affectionate cats in the county. What a different world we would live in if more of us put aside our harshness and our brusqueness towards our fellow human beings and learned to live and act with more gentleness.

Actions

Let's learn to live a gentle life, ladies and gentlemen:

» Reflect for a few minutes on whether your own perfectionism has led to you not being gentle with yourself, which then transfers to others. Journal about any areas that come to mind.

» Think of a person with whom you have been a little harsh and decide now to treat them with more gentleness. You may well see a change in them as well as yourself.

» Today, if you find your emotions rising in a particular situation, try pausing for a moment and then reacting with more gentleness than you would have done previously.

DAY 35 » **Curious**

Dictionary definition:

'Marked by desire to investigate and learn.'
Merriam-Webster Dictionary

Quotes:

'I am neither especially clever nor especially gifted. I am only very, very curious.'
Albert Einstein, German theoretical physicist

'I think, at a child's birth, if a mother could ask a fairy godmother to endow it with the most useful gift, that gift should be curiosity.'
Eleanor Roosevelt, American political activist

'What I have is a malevolent curiosity. That's what drives my need to write and what probably leads me to look at things a little askew. I do tend to take a different perspective from most people.'
David Bowie, English singer-songwriter

'Be less curious about people and more curious about ideas.'
Marie Curie, Polish physicist and chemist

Insights

There's a lovely story about a Kenyan teenager called Richard Turere. He is a Maasai living on the edge of Nairobi National Park, where zebras would regularly escape from the park and lions would chase them for the kill, but then kill the locals' cattle as well. The locals would kill the lions when they had a chance but knew this wasn't ideal for the tourist industry, from which they also benefited. Richard, like many small boys in Kenya, was given the job of looking after the cows. He tried to think of ways to protect the cows from the lions and first came up with the idea of lighting a fire but found that it helped the lions see the cattle in the cowshed. He next made a scarecrow, which worked for a day until the lions realised it didn't move and therefore wasn't human.

One day, when he was walking around with a torch, he worked out that the lions wouldn't come anywhere near him as they didn't like the moving light. Previously, his curiosity had led him to take apart his mum's radio and put it back together, and with his knowledge of electronics he created an elaborate device with wires, a transformer and lights that made it look like someone was walking with a torch around the outside of the cowshed. The lions stayed away and stayed alive, as did his family's cows. Richard remembers being a little boy and looking up into the sky, seeing an aeroplane and promising to himself that he would fly one day. On the basis that I saw Richard on YouTube giving a Ted Talk in the USA, I imagine he achieved that ambition too.

Curiosity often leads to creativity, and children have a wonderful curiosity that we often lose as we grow up, along with the creativity it brings. I remember my oldest son, Josh, hearing the phrase 'Mary laid Jesus in a manger' at Christmas and having a furrowed expression on his young brow for a while, before asking, 'Did the egg come out of Mary's bottom?' I almost renamed Josh 'Why' as that was the most common word he used. It could be exhausting trying to answer his questions, but he was only trying to fulfil his curiosity. He is now a very good computer programmer and puts that curiosity to work every day. It is important that the rest of us regain our childhood curiosity. Paul Lindley, founder of Ella's Kitchen, would call it 'growing down', learning to be like children again, as they generally get a lot more right than adults. Children are the epitome of the unconditioned self but as we grow older, experience failure and sometimes ridicule, we lose this curiosity and other child-like attributes that we would do very well to grow back down into.

When I was a little older than Richard Turere, with as much curiosity as him but less creativity, I once lit the huge gas tap at the front of the chemistry lab to see how big the flame was, before the teacher arrived for the chemistry lesson. The answer was at least three metres as it came close to singeing the tie of the boy at the other end of the workbench. Remarkably, when I mentioned that very story the other day on a podcast interview, I discovered that the interviewer had done exactly the same at his school. As we have both been relatively successful, then perhaps our curiosity could have been a factor? Most people, if asked to name a genius, would mention Albert Einstein, but he seems not to have thought of himself in this way – just as being very curious. And we read that David Bowie appreciated that his curiosity would be what led him to have a different perspective on life, although I am not sure that curiosity could ever be called malevolent. Could we go as far as to say that creativity is impossible without curiosity? Ask the poets, philosophers, artists, engineers, explorers and writers, and most would put down at least some of their success to curiosity.

We talked on Day 32 about being connected, but in relation to our connectivity with nature, it is curiosity that links us with nature in an amazing way. There are so many incredible constructions and behaviours in nature that even now, in the 21st century, we understand less than ten per cent of the whole picture, according to scientists. That should be enough to keep *Homo sapiens* curious for a long time yet.

Realising how important curiosity is, how do we bring it into the workplace and into our leadership? First, it is the not knowing that makes us good leaders. There is nothing worse than those who know it all and who aren't curious enough about another's perspective to want to find out more. The older I become, the more I realise how much I don't know – especially about other people – and the more I realise I can learn from those in our company who are a similar age to my children. Curiosity and an inquisitive nature mark the beginnings of wisdom. Realising that we know very little, and being curious about learning more, is the start of good leadership.

Second, as we have learned, curiosity is the foundation stone of creativity. Many great business ideas have come from an enquiry such as 'what if we tried it this way?' or 'what if we did something different here?' Ensuring that curiosity is encouraged within our companies and organisations will lead to everyone in the company putting creativity at the heart of what they do. More ideas will flow, and you never know, one of those ideas could be a complete game-changer.

Finally, curiosity makes us open people: open to new ideas, flexible and open-hearted to others, even when they appear very different to us. Curiosity rids us of fear and enables us to love those we may have

The Fourth Bottom Line

considered unlovable in the past. As a leader, being open to others is so important as we adapt to a world that is changing rapidly; we simply can't base our ideas on what worked ten years ago – or even last year. Being curious about new ideas will be the making of you. Curiosity may have killed the cat, but it brings us humans life – and abundance in that life.

Actions

Let's learn to be more curious today:

» Reflect for a few minutes now on how and where you could be more curious in your life. Could it be by changing what you read, changing who you listen to or doing something unusual for you in some other way?

» Think about something in nature or, if you can, go for a short walk and pick up a natural object and practise curiosity. What is it made of? How does it work? Why is it like that?

» In a meeting or conversation today, try to be more curious and ask more 'why' questions. As a leader, practise adopting the approach that others often know more than you do in different areas.

DAY 36 » **Contrite**

Dictionary definition:

'Feeling or showing sorrow and remorse for a sin or shortcoming.'
Merriam-Webster Dictionary

Quotes:

'What differentiates leaders is the ability to recover following a mistake. I make mistakes all the time, but I cop to them, apologize, and move on. Contrition is powerful.'
Dana Walden, American businesswoman

'There is a sacredness in tears. They are not the mark of weakness, but of power. They speak more eloquently than ten thousand tongues. They are the messengers of overwhelming grief, of deep contrition, and of unspeakable love.'
Washington Irving, American short-story writer

'When you realise you've made a mistake, take immediate steps to correct it.'
Dalai Lama, Tibetan spiritual leader

'Saying sorry doesn't solve the problem. It's what you do after that truly counts.'
Drake, Canadian rapper

Insights

This characteristic may seem like a slightly old-fashioned and possibly strange way to describe a good leader. In fact, I originally thought of using the word 'repentant' but that possibly has too many religious connotations of guilt for some people. The characteristic I am describing here is the ability of a leader to say sorry when they have screwed up. Particularly politicians, but also those in the business world, seem to think being sorry or contrite is a sign of weakness. This probably comes from the over-masculinised, competitive style of leadership that is overwhelmingly dominant and which generates thoughts such as: 'Don't show your enemy your weaknesses, they may pounce and destroy you.' The converse is true and showing no contrition is a sign of poor leadership and we must work hard to make being contrite, just like vulnerability, a sign of leadership strength rather than weakness. After all, people expect their leaders to be trustworthy and human, not perfect.

Those who apologise and mean it when they make mistakes are better leaders than those who find saying sorry difficult. I can recollect several occasions when a public figure (often a politician) has clearly done something wrong, yet refuses to apologise when pressed by journalists. Instead, they may come up with mitigation for their actions or may even hint at an apology, and then add a 'but...'. On these occasions, I have found myself shouting at the TV: 'Just say sorry!' Contrition would be so much better than making excuses for their actions and, in my view, would garner a much more favourable public response, making it politically the most expedient course of action. Yet often there is no contrition forthcoming, as pride and ego are difficult to step back from.

Clearly just saying the word 'sorry' is no good at all; we have to understand what we have done wrong before we utter the words and we should not say sorry without taking the time to understand our responsibility in the matter for which we are repentant. Even if we know there is fault on both sides, we can 100 per cent apologise for our faults without tagging a reason or excuse on to the end of our apology. All that does is cancel out the apology to those we are apologising to, so please don't do it! Offering a full apology for our part in causing hurt enables others to start the process of forgiveness. It is often not the end of that process, which may have to carry on for a while, depending on the depth and level of hurt caused, but true contrition opens the door for the process to at least start.

Contrition, however, is not just about the words; it is more about our actions following the words. As the rapper Drake has said, 'Saying sorry doesn't solve the problem. It's what you do after that truly counts.' We have all heard stories of the bully or abuser who continually says sorry but continues with his abusive behaviour. Their contrition may seem genuine, but clearly it is completely meaningless unless it is accompanied by a complete change in behaviour.

Take, for example, the CEO of a company who, in 2018 after some emails and protests emboldened by the #MeToo movement, apologised to the women within his business about the lack of female representation on the board and accompanying misogyny within the organisation. He apologised to everyone in the company at the next staff meeting, but a few months later, little has changed within the company – by which point dramatic action is required to back up his apology. He would have been better not uttering the apology in the first place, as it appeared meaningless. Those disempowered women, who initially felt some hope, came crashing down again and they would have done better to have moved in 2018 to a more enlightened company.

I strongly believe a leader's strength is also demonstrated by a sense of contrition for the impact that other people like her or him have had on others throughout history. For example, we might have a sense of sorrowfulness as a white person for the disempowerment that white people have historically caused to those of another skin colour. Showing a sense of contrition as today's representatives of what our ancestors have done is important for healing to come to the oppressed and for us to move towards a more equal society.

I have a very clear memory from an occasion when I was speaking to a group in Kenya, when I became side-tracked and started to describe a trip on which I had been part of a delegation to a different country to apologise for wrongdoing committed by the British Empire. As I started to tell the story of how I, as a British person, felt a degree of responsibility for what had been done by our forefathers many years ago, and how we had apologised on their behalf, I could hear people start to cry in the room where I was speaking. I stopped talking and asked the interpreter what was happening. He told me that only a few hundred metres from where we were standing, there had been a massacre of innocent local Kenyans by British soldiers. Of course, I changed my plans for the talk and went through a process of contrition and asking for forgiveness from the descendants of those massacred. It was so powerful and there were plenty of tears on both sides.

We might ask whether tears are really necessary for either personal or larger-scale apologies. I think that if you are free to express your sorrow with tears, it will certainly add weight to your apology; but if you do not readily cry, you can still make a wholehearted apology. With greater contrition, though, there are often more emotions. Crying can be a tremendous release on a personal level, but more important than any tears are a heart-felt apology offered with humility, followed by actions that seal the apology.

Our company held an environmental conference in May 2019, which was a great day of discussions about how we, as food and drink businesses, could make more of a difference in the world through running our organisations more sustainably; and many made pledges about what we were going to change both personally and within our businesses. I completed the day by talking about how our prevarication on acting against climate change in the West had already resulted in many people in poorer countries dying. By the end of the talk, more than 50 per cent of the delegates were crying, including me; and adding that emotion and those feelings of contrition to our pledges made for a powerful combination. In fact, we still received emails over a year later from people for whom that day was the start of their adopting a different attitude on environmental issues. That, to me, is true contrition: genuine sorrow with emotion followed by decisive restorative action.

Actions

Let's learn to be more contrite today:

» How easy do you find it to say sorry and mean it? In which situations do you find it easier and in which is it harder? Journal about whatever comes to mind.

» As a leader, to what extent do others view you as a contrite person? Do you perhaps give out a vibe that you are absolutely right and difficult to challenge? Reflect for a few moments on how others view you.

» Be keenly aware today of any situation in which you may have caused hurt recently at work or home, and demonstrate your contrition with restorative action.

DAY 37 » **Protective**

Dictionary definition:

'Wanting to protect someone from criticism, hurt, danger, etc. because you like them very much.'
Cambridge English Dictionary

Quotes:

'Protection and security are only valuable if they do not cramp life excessively.'
Carl Jung, Swiss psychiatrist

'Just imagine what would happen if your daughter was standing there. What would you do, how would you fight? So you have to join hands, you have to take each child as your daughter. Soon you will feel their sorrow and then you will feel the strength that comes out of you to protect them.'
Anuradha Koirala, Nepalese social activist

'God requires that we assist the animals, when they need our help. Each being (human or creature) has the same right of protection.'
St Francis of Assisi, Italian friar, mystic and preacher

'In this universe we all need to be protected and if we don't need any protection at all, it means that we are either dead or become a kind of god!'
Mehmet Murat İldan, Turkish author

Insights

If we surveyed people in the workplace and asked them whether they felt protected by their leaders, the results may well be disappointing in many organisations. Yet surely the most important job of a leader is to provide a haven, a secure place where people can be productive and not paralysed by fear. I am writing this during the Covid-19 pandemic where, in the UK, the government is currently doing a decent job of protecting people from fear by a furlough scheme, paying employers to keep their people on the payroll during the uncertainty. They are at home, not working, but, in effect, being paid by the government. I was talking to someone the other day who is being furloughed, but whose employer was claiming the money but forcing her to continue to work as normal at home. This is not only amoral but illegal, yet this individual was not prepared to shop their employer to HMRC for fear of being found out and losing her job. Not surprisingly, a few months ago this same company failed to protect its female employees when a sexist email went out from a director, who wasn't pulled up on his crass behaviour. How I would love to go into a business like that, get rid of these bad leaders and create a new, more protective culture!

Our traditional hierarchical, top-down view of leadership simply doesn't help us here. I have mentioned previously that I would never use the traditional organogram with leaders at the top of a tree but would much prefer one where the leaders were underneath and supporting those above them. Leaders for whom status is too important are seldom protective leaders, more thinking of their own position than that of other's security. Often due to their own insecurity, those who should protect create a culture of fear and bullying, which can create a completely toxic place to work. We might not expect that these types of cultures would still exist, as there are so many other great places to work, yet I recently read the following comment posted online in 2020 under a piece about my previous book, *Forces for Good*:

> I have spent the last 2 years in the zombie company – that was a truly abnormal place full of great people but some of them were dangerous paranoid psychopaths. The place where naive people were wasting their time with no clue what is really going on behind the glass doors. I witnessed how [the] company is literally wasting money and never try to invest into people (no trainings, no promotion). The company where people were bullied and harassed, neglected and ignored – not able

to openly speak out theirs [*sic*] mind about wrongdoing and about ideas. I am so happy not working there anymore.

In the 21st century, I find this absolutely astonishing and was not surprised to learn that the writer of this post had left the company for his own wellbeing. Moving away from those who are meant to protect us, yet who aren't doing so, is often the right step to take.

A few leaders have always been in it for themselves and are simply not very nice people. They climb the corporate or political ladder, scheming and conniving their way to the top in the relentless pursuit of power, always making themselves and their position their main priority. These people permanently operate from their conditioned self and more than likely experienced some childhood deficit in a big way. There are others who start with genuine motives and wanting to do good things, but who become distanced from their own organisation, which can create an unprotective atmosphere for the people who work there. I am embarrassed to say that this happened within my own company many years ago, due to my own lack of awareness. Owing to rapid growth, I had over-delegated responsibility to other managers and a couple of individuals had set up their own little fiefdoms of power, with fear ruling the people under their poor management. Once I found out what was going on, these were broken up and I had to apologise to those who had experienced this awful unprotective management within my own business. I'll be honest that I struggle to understand why anyone would behave like that; surely it creates a happier life for them and the people under them without the strife, but such is the drive for power in some individuals that they cannot see beyond themselves. It is dangerous and common; as the old saying goes: 'Power corrupts; absolute power corrupts absolutely.'

So, how do we become a real protector as a leader? First, declare your intention to protect your people. State that you are there for them in all eventualities and if they ever feel unprotected, they need to come and talk to you about it. Second, check in with your people and find out if they are comfortable and happy at work. Ask whether you can do anything to make their work environment a happier and better place to be. As CEO, I try to check in with everyone from time to time, even if I am not their direct line manager. If you have the right managers in place, who are interested in protecting their people, they won't be threatened by this or feel that you are undermining their authority. If you have managers around who are threatened by this sort of approach, they probably haven't created the right culture around them. I remember talking to Bob Moore, Founder and CEO of Bob's Red Mill, over dinner once, and he told me that every day he would walk around the factory floor and chat with the people there, all 200 of them. He not only knew all their names, but also the names of their children and their pets too! Finally, if ever anything arises that compromises that sense of protection, you must step in and deal with it immediately, without delay. One of my managers asked me the other day whether they should ring a customer to tell them that their behaviour towards one of her team was unacceptable and if they carried on like that again, they wouldn't be a customer. She was concerned, as there had been a completely unnecessary and undeserved torrent of abuse on the phone to a new member of her team. I, of course, said 'yes' as the employee needs to feel that we as a company are protecting them – and as a result I expect the customer has behaved better since. The customer isn't always right.

There is such a thing as overprotection, of course, and we are all familiar with mothers and fathers who are overprotective of their kids and don't allow them to develop their own wings and fly the nest. Apart from anything else, this can cause issues when these offspring enter adult relationships. The same is true with the work equivalents of mums and dads, the managers. If we are overprotective of our work kids, then they won't mature and learn to make their own decisions. People need to make mistakes in order to learn and the key to good protective leadership in the work environment is to push them out of the nest, yet at the same time create a good safety net in case they fall. I remember the first time I heard how eagles teach their young to fly. They literally do push the eaglets out of the nest high up on a cliff face and then fly out with them. When the fledglings lose confidence and start to fall towards the earth, the eagles swoop under them and let them land on their backs. Then they take them back up and start again. What a great image, illustrating what it is to be a protective leader!

Actions

As a leader, think about how you can better protect others in your team:

» Now, of course, you may not have felt protected as a child yourself, which can sometimes make this difficult. So first reflect for a few moments on how protected you felt when you were younger – or indeed now. Journal any notes and, if necessary, you may benefit from talking therapy about any arising issues.

» If, as a leader, you haven't ever told your people that you are there to protect them and create a safe environment for them to work in, physically and psychologically, then do this today or at the next team meeting.

» This week, spend some time checking in with people at work about their wellbeing. Ask them how happy they are at work, and what could be improved.

DAY 38 » **Intuitive**

Dictionary definition:

'(Knowledge from) an ability to understand or know something immediately based on your feelings rather than facts.'
Cambridge English Dictionary

Quotes:

'The intuitive mind is a sacred gift and the rational mind is a faithful servant. We have created a society that honours the servant and has forgotten the gift.'
Albert Einstein, German theoretical physicist

'I think women have an innate ability to be intuitive with people that they truly love, but they have to trust that inner voice, and I think it is there. I think we are more intuitive than men.'
Andie MacDowell, American actress

'Listen to the wind, it talks. Listen to the silence, it speaks. Listen to your heart, it knows.'
Native American proverb

'Have the courage to follow your heart and intuition. They somehow already know what you truly want to become. Everything else is secondary.'
Steve Jobs, American entrepreneur

Insights

Growing up in the seventies and eighties, I was always taught to trust my head and not my heart or gut, the former being the centre of our rational being and the latter two often referred to as being governed by our intuitive mind. However, I have always disobeyed the teaching of my younger years and predominantly made decisions intuitively. In fact, the occasions when I have made poor decisions are when I have trusted my rational mind more than my intuition. I remember when we were launching a brand called Heaven's Kitchen, and we had been working with a third-party manufacturer on the project, about whom I had always had a nagging feeling of negativity. However, we persevered with the project, as on paper they were the ideal partner and ticked all the right boxes. A range of three products was created and I went to the factory for the first production run, still with a slightly gloomy feeling around the project, despite the seeming outward success. Within two weeks of the launch, the manufacturer had gone into administration and our project was dying, leaving me with an increased mortgage on the house and nothing to show for it. If I had trusted my intuition rather than, or in addition to, my rational mind, there would inevitably have been a better outcome.

None of us purely operate from our rational mind, whether we know it or not, and everyone is intuitive to a greater or lesser degree. Women perhaps more so than men, although both sexes in the West probably have a reduced intuition due to the overemphasis placed during our education on working from our brain's cerebral cortex; we hardly educate the whole child in the UK, do we? We will discuss how to train ourselves to be more intuitive a little later, but some recent interesting research at Harvard Medical School has shown that our gut and our brain are in constant communication, and indeed the enteric nervous system that regulates our gut is often called the body's second brain. Braden Kuo's paper states that, 'Although it can't compose poetry or solve equations, this extensive network [enteric nervous system] uses the same chemicals and cells as the brain to help us digest and alert the brain when something is amiss. Gut and brain are in constant communication.' Ancient Eastern medical practitioners didn't need Harvard to tell them this; their medical and meditation practices have been helping people listen to their gut for many millennia.

Rather than referring to a gut feeling when talking about intuition, some people use slightly different language and say that they were led by their heart. However, they are usually thinking of the limbic part of the brain, the seat of our emotions where many of our neurochemicals are produced. I would not actually have believed my physical heart was involved if I used this expression, but remarkably there does appear to be an emotional intelligence connected to the heart. As with the gut, the heart and brain are in constant communication and our emotions can be affected by the heart and vice versa. There is even some evidence that the emotional intelligence and tastes of heart transplant patients can be altered after their operations. In 2013, *Medical Daily* reported that there were changes in the tastes and preferences of those receiving heart transplants linked to those from whom the donor heart came. This extraordinary study, albeit from a small sample of ten patients, found parallels in food, music, art, sexual, recreational and career preferences between the heart donor and the transplant recipient. In a further extraordinary example, one patient receiving a heart from someone who was killed by a gunshot to the face reported having dreams involving hot flashes of light to his face.

Now this is completely mind-blowing material for our Western mindset and there is clearly much more research to be done on both the gut and heart. Some would say that this type of activity is simply part and parcel of the right-sided brain, but maybe we should lean to the East and listen to the ancient practices. For now, let's agree there are aspects of intelligence away from our thinking brain, the cerebrum, so let's look at how we can awaken our intuition through learning to listen to them.

In some respects, many of the characteristics we are aiming to develop within ourselves in these pages will be helped by developing our intuition, and many of the practices I have talked about will help to do this, such as those of solitude and silence. Many of us aren't used to listening to our intuition because we are surrounded by noise – sometimes physical, but more often mental noise. It is difficult to intuit if we are always thinking of the past few hours or future hours or days. It is essential to quieten ourselves down, go for a walk or simply sit and learn to *be* without *doing* anything. Meditation is a process in which we quieten down that internal noise and I would recommend this as a daily practice for 10 to 15 minutes at least. I find the start of the day the best time for me; but in the middle of the day, you might be able to take time out and practise mindfulness, which may provide an energising break during the day.

Breathing deep into our gut and being aware of our physical body may help develop intuition; it is almost as if we are moving our activity from our head into our stomach or our heart. Another tip is to listen to our emotions: sometimes when we feel drained and exhausted, it is because we are pushing against what we think in our heads we should be doing, as our gut or heart has different ideas. Daydreams or dreams at night may be our intuitive self talking to us. Be aware too, as you go through each day, of any experiences, events or even creatures in nature that may be expressing something to you. It's all about listening to the world around us rather than the words we hear. At the start of many of our meetings at Cotswold Fayre, we start with silence and by inhaling some deep breaths, and occasionally even some physical stretching exercises. As a result, because we are not only in our minds, we have better, more intuitive, more effective meetings.

Now, for some people this may sound a little farfetched and I can't claim to understand how it all works. However, it is interesting to note that I read through over 100 quotes on intuition to choose four for this chapter, and these include insights from scientists such as Einstein; in fact, I discovered more than five from him alone on intuition. We think of scientists as those people who use the rational parts of their brains the most, but it appears that they are among the strongest advocates for developing our intuition. Let's finish this section by repeating the quote from that modern-day genius Steve Job: 'Have the courage to follow your heart and intuition. They somehow already know what you truly want to become. Everything else is secondary.'

Actions

Let's aim to be a little more intuitive today:

» First, reflect on how intuitive you are: do you need to have worked everything out in your brain, or are you happy going along with your heart or gut feelings? Journal what comes to mind.

» Let's start to understand the heart and gut. Breathe deeply into your body with your hands on your stomach. After a while, do the same with your hand on your heart. Appreciate those different parts of our body and how we may be guided by other areas than our cerebral cortex.

» In your meetings today, and even when working alone, while you are thinking, build in a pause to listen to your body separately from your brain.

DAY 39 » **Non-judgmental**

Dictionary definition:

'Of, relating to, or denoting an attitude, approach, etc., that is open and not incorporating a judgment one way or the other.'
Collins English Dictionary

Quotes:

'Any judgment is past oriented, and existence is always herenow, life is always herenow. All judgments are coming from your past experiences, your education, your religion, your parents – which may be dead, but their judgments are being carried by your mind and they will be given as a heritage to your children. Generation after generation, every disease is being transferred as a heritage. Only a non-judgmental mind has intelligence, because it is spontaneously responding to reality.'
Rajneesh, Indian mystic

'The secret of happiness is love and secret of love is non-judgmental care.'
Debasish Mridha, American physician and philosopher

'It's very easy to be judgmental until you know someone's truth.'
Kate Winslet, English actress

'Simply put, mindfulness is moment-to-moment non-judgmental awareness.'
Jon Kabat-Zinn, American professor

Insights

Being judgmental potentially creates one of the greatest obstacles to our achieving higher levels of many of the characteristics we are hoping to grow into in these pages. It is difficult to be judgmental and at the same time be humble, compassionate or even joyful; yet for many of us a horrible tendency to judge is almost built into us. I have talked about the conditioned self and the unconditioned self throughout; and our judgment comes very much from our conditioned self. Our judgments come from what has been instilled in us from our parents, our education, our culture, our upbringing or even our bad experiences with a particular type of person. This means that we judge other people and tar them with a certain brush before we really know them. Judgmentalism is a pernicious disease and very few have rid themselves of all of its symptoms.

Even when we think we are making progress, we should realise we still have a way to go. A while ago I met someone at a social event who went to a very well-known public school where many politicians seem to hail from. While I was at Oxford University, I knew several people from this particular school and due to a couple of unfortunate interactions that didn't show them in the best light, I wrote them all off as being equally rude and objectionable. I have run across several people from that school since and, to my shame, have always pre-judged them unfairly. This example from 2019 was no exception; I had a superficial conversation with this man around the dinner table and upon leaving we exchanged business cards. A few days later I received an email. He had clearly checked me out online and read about my first book, *Forces for Good*, and the subject had resonated with him. We met again and formed a deep connection over how essential it is for a business to completely change its modus operandi in order to put social and environmental change higher than profit.

It hit me for a few days how many opportunities I had missed prior to that moment to connect with people due to my own prejudices; probably many, which was chastening. Our judgment often melts away once we get to know people, which it did for me in the above example – which shows just how crazy it is to judge people without getting to know them. In effect, you are saying that they look and seem a bit like a person who wasn't very nice to you, so you're not going to bother getting to know them and will just assume that all people that remind you of a particular person all fit the same stereotype. Much of our judgmentalism is a defence mechanism used to protect our ego; that is exactly what conditioned behaviour is: ego-protecting behaviour. There are various reasons we act like this: we may be trying to make ourselves feel superior to others, thereby giving us a false sense of worth; we may be avoiding our own faults by pointing them out in others; or we may be protecting ourselves from being hurt by others.

So how do we become less judgmental? First, as much of this has to do with low self-esteem, self-acceptance is a good start and will help us accept others. We are not perfect and never will be, so learning to accept ourselves, warts and all, will help to prevent us from being so judgmental. Second, judgmentalism is often an instant reaction, so if we learn to curb that first reaction, we will learn more about the other person; for example, perhaps we will learn that they are unfriendly because they too are hurting from the actions of others in the past. Learning to stop our knee-jerk reactions allows us to see beneath the surface of a fellow human-being, and we may then start to feel compassion rather than judgment. Third, without judging yourself too much, you can learn to be critical of your judgmentalism and tell yourself that you can never fully know the story of another human being, and if you had experienced similar circumstances you would almost certainly have turned out worse than them!

Learning to live in the present moment will also help us relieve ourselves of our judgmentalism. That is essentially what mindfulness is: moment by moment non-judgmentalism. Through mindfulness, we can learn to stand outside ourselves, detach ourselves from our judgments and observe them as if from a distance. We don't have to have an opinion about everything around us, anyway. The Dalai Lama said, 'Love is the absence of judgment', so practising love, empathy, kindness and compassion towards others will be a sure-fire way of moving on from judgment.

It is difficult to build good relationships or be good leaders if we are judgmental, because we will end up receiving an edited version of others, as they won't want to share their true selves with us since they don't want us to judge them. Because of this, judgmental people often aren't told the truth and don't have their opinions challenged, leading the judgmental person to think they are 100 per cent right, which can end up making them even worse. It's a vicious circle we would do well to escape; two people protecting their own egos is a disaster waiting to happen, so learn to be the better person and let go of your judgments with love and compassion. That love will then allow the other person to let go of their own judgments and enable them to be who they really are too. I'm not saying this is easy to do, far from it, but it will bring healing and connection into relationships, which, as human beings, is what we all crave deep down.

Now, there is a difference between being judgmental and judging. It is sometimes right to judge and call out actions that are clearly wrong in anyone's moral code. The important factors in this type of judging are that we are not second-guessing people's motivations or being hypocritical. Going back to our self-acceptance, we are often judgmental with others about the things we don't like about ourselves. So, we can call others out on what they are doing *only* if we are aware that we are working on our own issues too, and our motivation is to help the other person, not to make ourselves better than them in our own eyes.

Returning to Rajneesh's quote, we have a great opportunity to remove judgmentalism from our lineage. We don't want to pass that on to our children, our friendship group or even our workplace, do we? So let's move into a more compassionate, loving world with less judgment.

Actions

Let's start today to be less judgmental of ourselves and others:

» Begin by reflecting in quiet for a few moments on what leads you to be judgmental. Do you really accept yourself properly, even the bad bits? Are you passing on your harshness with yourself to others?

» Think of the type of person you tend to judge. Write a list of the positive attributes likely to be present in those types of people.

» Make a habit of offering compassion rather than judgment to those you meet today even if they are people you don't naturally warm to.

DAY 40 » **Self-disciplined**

Dictionary definition:

'Someone who is self-disciplined has the ability to control themselves and to make themselves work hard or behave in a particular way without needing anyone else to tell them what to do.'
Collins English Dictionary

Quotes:

'For a man to conquer himself is the first and noblest of all victories.'
Plato, Greek philosopher

'Mastering others is strength. Mastering yourself is true power.'
Lao Tzu, Chinese philosopher

'The one quality which sets one man apart from another – the key which lifts one to every aspiration while others are caught up in the mire of mediocrity – is not talent, formal education, nor intellectual brightness – it is self-discipline. With self-discipline all things are possible. Without it, even the simplest goal can seem like the impossible dream.'
Theodore Roosevelt, former president of the United States

'In reading the lives of great men, I found that the first victory they won was over themselves... self-discipline with all of them came first.'
Harry S. Truman, former president of the United States

Insights

There's a well-known story of a man who went to a tattooist, as he had always wanted a tattoo of a lion on his back. The tattooist started tattooing the tail of the lion and the man cried out in pain, asking the tattooist what he was doing. When the tattooist replied that he was doing the tail as requested, the man said he would have a lion without a tail. Next, the tattooist started on the lion's whiskers and the man again cried out in pain and asked the tattooist what he was doing. When the tattooist replied that he was doing the whiskers, the man said he would have a lion without whiskers. The next area the tattooist started to draw was the back and again the man cried out. This time the tattooist threw down his tools and threw the man out of his shop, shouting after him, 'How can you expect to get what you want without a little discomfort?'

I was initially going to use the word 'ascetic' today, but it is not a word used in common parlance these days. It also carries with it a sense of severe self-discipline and is often used for those in religious orders, such as monks, whether Buddhists or Christians. This may have seemed a little too much in this context, but the aims of those in religious orders who put their pupils through the hardship of denial of what the rest of us would call life's essentials are very similar to what I want to convey here. The word 'ascetic' is derived from the Greek for training or exercise and in some respects is similar to the word 'discipline' which comes from Latin and means 'penitential chastisement; punishment for the sake of correction'. Looking at the roots of these two words, the word 'ascetical' now perhaps seems less harsh than 'self-disciplined'. But both words carry with them the sense of tough personal measures in order to change us into better people. Monks go without the physical 'needs' of sleep, clothes, food, conversation and sex, with the aim of heightening their spiritual awareness. And we may want to do without some of those necessities too for shorter periods; but even if we are only interested in mental development rather than spiritual, there is an aspect of doing without the basics that will sharpen up our minds. Those who always respond to their physical desires are not destined for greatness. As Plato said, 'For a man to conquer himself is the first and noblest of all victories.'

Achieving our long-term goal of building an organisation or becoming very good at anything will always involve sometimes saying 'no' to pleasures that are not wrong in and of themselves, but just wrong for us at that time. In the start-up days of Cotswold Fayre, I was also engaged in working long days in the local community and would come home and have to start work again, putting orders together and hand-writing invoices until around 4 am, before filling the van up with diesel and leaving it for a friend, who would start work at 6 am as a delivery driver. Occasionally I did this myself after two hours' sleep; not good practice, but sometimes hard work just has to be done. Self-discipline is about much more than hard work, though. It may sometimes be about choosing not to drink any alcohol the night before a big presentation the following day. It may mean watching less TV or social media, turning your phone off for several hours and doing some studying. For example, recently I was asked to do a talk on a subject matter that I had some knowledge of, but not one I felt I knew enough about, so I set aside hour blocks late each day to read three books on the subject to improve my knowledge. This is time I might have otherwise spent watching TV during the evening.

Everything I am writing about here needs to be balanced with the lessons offered in the self-care chapter, as there is a fine line between the two. Your personality will often determine which side of that line you naturally fall on. It does us good to eat well at regular times and have enough sleep; but self-discipline is about appreciating when it is right to completely relax and enjoy life and when we could be improving ourselves by doing the opposite and withholding from ourselves certain physical 'needs'. As you will know by now, I would certainly recommend carving out time at the beginning of each day to meditate, read and create a sense of calm before launching into the day. Yes, this will require jumping out of bed earlier than you would otherwise, but you will gain energy by starting the day in a beneficial way.

The important thing here is to find our own niche. What is right for one person is not necessarily right for another and there are certainly no rules, as these risk becoming a form of bondage rather than offering the path to freedom. It is about self-control and not being a slave to our physical appetites. Do you imagine that a professional athlete absolutely loves getting up early and train every day? They may well do 90 per cent of the time, but 10 per cent of the time they would much rather be doing something else; yet these excelling sportspeople train harder on the difficult days than on others – and that's why they are the best. It's the same with us: do activities such as exercise or mental training on the days when you don't want to – that is the core of self-discipline.

We often look at other people and wish we had their musical gifts, their leadership gifts, their speaking or writing talent, or even their software expertise. While there are a few absurdly gifted people out there who are naturally very good without much effort, the vast majority of them became very good at what they do through an absurd amount of practice. K. Anders Ericsson, a psychologist, was the first to suggest that to master anything required 10,000 hours of practice: that means two hours a day for nearly fourteen years. Whether this specific length of time is true or not, masters in anything often practise their craft for far longer than others who are naturally more *gifted* – and, as a result, end up surpassing them with their success. In one of our quotes today, Roosevelt talks about self-discipline being what distinguishes those who excel and lift themselves out of mediocrity. Many people are stuck in the valley of mediocrity and haven't got the self-discipline to climb out of the valley and up into the mountains.

Why is it that physical abstinence helps sharpen our spiritual and mental sides? I am not sure that anyone has answered that in totality, but one thing I am sure about is that many of us in the West give pre-eminence to the physical above the other two aspects, so haven't explored the full realm of self-discipline. We would consider it very strange to miss a meal or go without food for a day, but in the Eastern traditions and the more ascetic traditions of all types, abstinence is not considered strange. The important thing is that it doesn't become legalistic. We must go with our intuition and what seems right for the occasion. Often, though, a new clarity of mind and direction comes when we bring a greater level of self-discipline into our lives. Mastering ourselves is indeed true power and will certainly make us better leaders and better people.

Actions

Live a life of self-discipline today and all days:

» Reflect for a few moments on your levels of self-discipline. Ask yourself how disciplined you are. When you are down or feeling low, do you binge on food, drink or TV, or do something more positive?

» Perhaps today think of something physical you could forego in order to sharpen the mental or spiritual sides of yourself. I'm reluctant to suggest anything here – it has to be what is right for you.

» Are there any practices you could build into your life on a longer-term basis, such as exercise, meditation or a time in which to read something inspirational every day?

DAY 41 » **Wise**

Dictionary definition:

'Having the ability to discern or judge what is true, right, or lasting; sagacious.'
Free Dictionary

Quotes:

'And yet the wiser mind mourns less for what age takes away than what it leaves behind.'
William Wordsworth, English romantic poet

'To acquire knowledge, one must study; but to acquire wisdom, one must observe.'
Marilyn vos Savant, American author and playwright

'Yesterday I was clever, so I wanted to change the world. Today I am wise, so I am changing myself.'
Rumi, Persian poet

'Wisdom tends to grow in proportion to one's awareness of one's ignorance.'
Anthony de Mello, Indian Jesuit priest and psychotherapist

Insights

Socrates never wrote any of his thinking down, so much of what we know about what he said comes from what his follower Plato wrote down at his trial, during which Socrates uttered, 'I am wiser than this man, for neither of us appears to know anything great and good; but he fancies he knows something although he knows nothing; whereas I, as I do not know anything, so I do not fancy I do.' In other words, if you think you know a lot, you are not wise! I had a Zoom meeting with an old friend recently, whom I hadn't seen for around ten years, and we were exploring what had changed for each of us during the intervening period. We both agreed that we thought we knew less than we did years before; as we had both become older, the more we realised what we didn't know. Certainly, when I was younger I thought I knew a lot – and, like many younger people, I let others know all about my great knowledge, probably to their great annoyance.

Many confuse intelligence with wisdom when the two are completely different. Zat Rana wrote an excellent article on 'Medium', a social journalism website, in which he explored the difference between intelligence and wisdom. He says intelligence is about knowing something, whereas wisdom is not only about knowing but understanding. Knowing relates to facts and how those facts apply to a certain situation, whereas wisdom carries with it a broader sense and is more fluid. With wisdom, we perceive the essence behind the knowledge and can see how this relates to other areas, along with its nuances and contradictions.

This fluidity of wisdom in applying knowledge comes from our life experiences; hence the association with older people being wise. I am amazed when I hear of autobiographies written by celebrities who are in their twenties and thirties; I am not sure whether anyone less than halfway through their life has any wisdom to pass on to others. They may have gained a huge amount of knowledge but simply have not experienced enough of life to apply the fluidity of a deeper understanding.

This morning, I listened to a podcast which was an hour-long interview with Jo Malone, a British perfumer. Jo is a few years older than me, so definitely well past the halfway point of her life, and as I listened, despite her claiming on the podcast that she wasn't particularly intelligent, wisdom seemed to ooze from her every pore. It is no coincidence that Jo has had a difficult life, having severe dyslexia and having had to leave school at age 13 to look after her mum who had suffered a stroke. Later in life she was diagnosed with an aggressive form of breast cancer, from which she completely recovered – although losing her sense of smell for a time, catastrophic to a perfumer. It is through difficult and testing experiences of life that knowledge metamorphoses into wisdom, and those who have suffered the most are often the wisest people around.

It is easy to think of our negative experiences as stopping us from achieving our purpose in life, or, at the very least, slowing us down, yet it is precisely these that develop us into the unique person we are and which help us build wisdom. I finally started to understand this fairly recently – that's how unwise I am! I had previously believed that a broken first marriage, a nearly destroyed business and several other bad experiences meant my life had completely gone off-track. Of course, there would have been ways in which all those negative experiences could have had better outcomes, but I finally understood that those experiences had helped form the person I am now and enriched my ability to contribute to other people's lives. In fact, I had the words 'it's time to be wise' rattling around in my head at the end of 2018. On the afternoon of New Year's Day, 2019, I went for a walk with my wife, a walk that we had enjoyed many times, and we heard a commotion of birds in the trees ahead, mocking an owl which swooped out and over our heads. And what is the owl commonly used as a symbol of – yes, wisdom! While I clearly still have much to learn, I took this sign as an encouragement to use my words more to help others, which I have tried to do more of since, although I still know far less than I used to! To be clear, I'm not sure we will ever relish negative experiences, but I can see clearly now how what seems negative at the time can be very positive in shaping us into better and wiser people for the future. Coming to that perspective while within a difficult time is a good indication of wisdom.

Another aspect that those in many other cultures can teach us in the West is veneration and respect for the older members of our communities. In our Western culture, we tend to treat our elder citizens as an inconvenience, or at best a distraction, and do not give them the respect they deserve. In many other cultures, elders are treated as the wise people that they truly are, and children and youths are taught to look up to and respect them. The younger members of society go to the matriarch or patriarch when they have a difficult moral dilemma, or are in some difficulty, and they expect to receive a wise answer. We would be a better and more flourishing society if all our older citizens were given this level of honour. In business too, while the younger ones may know far more than their elders in certain areas, a respect for those who have been running different businesses for years is healthy and there is wisdom there to be learned there. Let's not forget that in our celebration of youthful zeal.

The story most told about wisdom is that of King Solomon, to whom two women came one day, each laying claim to be the mother of a child. Rather than forensically examining the evidence, finding out who the father was or asking the neighbours, Solomon easily resolved the dispute by ordering the child to be cut in two. As this was about to be actioned, the real mother gave up her claim, saying that she would rather the child was given to the other woman. Instantly, Solomon declared that the woman who had offered to give up the child was the actual mother. Wisdom cuts straight to the core of the issue, isn't necessarily accompanied by lots of words and often sees a problem in a different way to others. That is the difference between knowledge and wisdom. As Solomon himself said, 'Wisdom is supreme; therefore, get wisdom. Though it cost all you have, get understanding.'

Actions

Becoming wise takes a lifetime, but today:

» Make a start by reflecting on what you consider to be the more negative experiences you have had in life and be thankful for the wisdom they have granted you. Ask yourself whether you are more able to see the positive in dark times than you used to do?

» As Marilyn vos Savant said, wisdom is not about studying but observing. Are there other, wiser people you know, or know of, whom you could spend some time with and learn from? Many would be pleased to guide you.

» Likewise, if you are past the midpoint of life, are there any others to whom you pass on wisdom? If you don't think you have anything to offer, that's the qualification test passed!

DAY 42 » **Loving**

Dictionary definition:

'Feeling, showing, or indicating love and affection.'
Collins English Dictionary

Quotes:

'Intense love does not measure, it just gives.'
Mother Teresa, Albanian-Indian missionary

'The moment you have in your heart this extraordinary thing called love and feel the depth, the delight, the ecstasy of it, you will discover that for you the world is transformed.'
Jiddu Krishnamurti, Indian speaker and writer

'Agape is disinterested love... Agape does not begin by discriminating between worthy and unworthy people, or any qualities people possess. It begins by loving others for their sakes... Therefore, agape makes no distinction between friend and enemy; it is directed toward both.'
Martin Luther King, Jr., American civil rights activist

'Immature love says: "I love you because I need you." Mature love says: "I need you because I love you."'
Erich Fromm, German social psychologist

Insights

'Love' and the ability to be 'loving' are broad terms, so let me define what I mean here in the context of leadership. First, the word 'love' is generally used with those we know rather than those we do not. We have looked at being compassionate elsewhere in this book, and the word 'compassion' is generally used for the feeling towards others who are suffering, carrying with it the desire to alleviate their suffering. Love, on the other hand, is a feeling of affection for those we know well. The ancient Greeks had four words for love: *storge* was used for familial love and affection of a parent to a child or vice versa; *philia* was used for the love in nonsexual friendship; *eros* was sexual love and attraction; and, finally, *agape* was the pure, unconditional kind of love.

It is the latter *agape* type of love that I will focus on here, which as the purist love carries through into the other three types of love and will make the other loves deeper and more enriching too. It is the *agape* type of love that makes us better political or business leaders. It is a great shame in this day and age that people rarely talk about love for others without there being sexual connotations of some kind: it is high time to redeem the word 'love' and to be able to describe ourselves as loving leaders without any sexual innuendos. In fact, over the past two years I have used the word love when speaking to other business leaders without any embarrassment. There is a sense of the transcendent about the fourth type of love as described by C. S. Lewis in his book *The Four Loves*. Lewis says the other three loves can be talked about in the terms of 'need-loves', whereas agape is a 'gift-love' that takes the people we love to another level. Of course, bringing the unconditional gift-love of agape into our love for family, friends and lovers will take all those relationships onto a higher level too.

Let's consider how we bring love into our leadership within our business or organisation. To talk about love in a work context only a few years ago would probably have resulted in comments about us being hippies or that we had lost it and had gone 'all new age'. It would have certainly also made the HR department a little nervous. Thank God we seem to have moved on, as I believe it is important to be able to love the people we lead. For many people, the workplace is the most important community in their lives, and as a result, leaders within the workplace are the modern-day equivalent to the village elders from the pre-industrial era. Many think that loneliness will become an even greater scourge as we move through the 21st century – and being loved within the workplace will become even more important. I've already discussed (on Day 37) removing the culture of fear by being a protective leader and ensuring there is a positive atmosphere with no fear. What better way to assuage fear than creating a culture of love in the workplace? Resetting culture and company DNA is helped by leaders learning to love their people.

Now, the great news about creating a loving culture is that it increases happiness, which in turn inspires excellent performances and results in more successful organisations. In addition, being a loving leader creates a better team dynamic with everyone rooting for each other, rather than trying to catch each other out and wanting to look better than them. What's more, creating a loving culture will reduce stress in the workplace and increase positive mental health and wellbeing. So why wouldn't you? Some would think that being loving is too wishy-washy a concept, that productivity will decrease and less work will get done as people fawn over each other around the coffee machine. However, they are wrong. The drive for people to do well comes from internal motivation. People don't need to be continually exhorted to perform and driven by external performance indicators; if they know they are loved and love coming to work, they will be more excited about achieving excellent results and will go the second mile for their colleagues which makes for much better teamwork and productivity. It really isn't rocket science, is it? So, let's look practically at how we can love our people.

One way of viewing this is to imagine your work colleagues as children. This isn't to belittle them, but the same loving behaviour that children need from their parents is exactly what people need in their workplace. Children love to be appreciated when they have achieved a goal and love to be encouraged during the process of completing a task. We know children need boundaries and so do our work colleagues; being clear about what we are expecting from them and what we are not expecting helps enormously. Helping people not to feel overwhelmed is part of loving them, and so is putting your arm around them (met-aphorically or not – up to you) and giving them the support that they need when they feel they can't cope. Children like nothing more than their parent's attention, so ensure that there are clear and open spaces when everyone can communicate exactly what they are feeling and thinking. Creating a family environment will enable people to be honest and authentic in their communication.

In our company, as mentioned, we often start our meetings with a period of quiet for a few minutes and a 'check-in' – when those present can let everyone else know how they are feeling at that moment. Initially, this might be in just a couple of words but sometimes we go into more detail. People are free to talk about work or personal stuff without fear of judgment, and this helps set the atmosphere of love and acceptance. Talking of home life, what better way to show love as a leader than giving people at work help with their difficulties at home? This might mean helping your people sort out a childcare problem, or it may mean providing bereavement counselling when someone has lost a relative or it could be resourcing financial counselling when colleagues have money troubles. Because the sense of community has been lost for many and they do not know where to look when in trouble, part of being a loving leader is to help create that loving community around them.

I can't think of a better way to finish today's thoughts than to reflect on the words that we have heard many times at wedding services, by far the most popular reading chosen by brides and grooms, the Apostle Paul's words to the Corinthians. As you read these words, please think of your leadership in these terms:

> Love suffers long and is kind; love does not envy; love does not parade itself, is not puffed up; does not behave rudely, does not seek its own, is not provoked, thinks no evil; does not rejoice in iniquity, but rejoices in the truth; bears all things, believes all things, hopes all things, endures all things.

What a great way to demonstrate love through all these qualities, as we seek to become more loving in our leadership.

Actions

Join me in learning to be more loving today:

» Read through those words from Paul again and, as you read them, reflect on whether your leadership been loving in that way? Journal any thoughts.

» How loving is your own workplace culture? What more could you do to foster love for the people there?

» Appreciate, encourage, support. Do one or all three of these today to show love to someone else who you think needs it.

DAY 43 » **Justice-loving**

Dictionary definition:

'Justice: fairness in the way people are dealt with.'
Cambridge English Dictionary

Quotes:

'I am going to fight capitalism even if it kills me. It is wrong that people like you should be comfortable and well fed while all around you people are starving.'
Sylvia Pankhurst, English suffragette

'Justice will not be served until those who are unaffected are as outraged as those who are.'
Benjamin Franklin, British-American polymath

'True peace is not merely the absence of tension: it is the presence of justice.'
Martin Luther King, Jr., American civil rights activist

'If you are neutral in situations of injustice, you have chosen the side of the oppressor. If an elephant has its foot on the tail of a mouse and you say that you are neutral, the mouse will not appreciate your neutrality.'
Desmond Tutu, South African cleric and theologian

Insights

On 1 December 1955, Rosa Parks, a Black African American, refused to stand up on a bus in Montgomery, Alabama so a white person could sit down. As everyone knows, this sparked the start of the Montgomery bus boycott, which lasted 382 days and led to the civil rights movement in the USA, which continues today. Rosa herself said, 'I had no idea history was being made. I was just tired of giving up.' We still live in a hugely unequal society, where there is a massive amount of injustice for billions of people in the world. According to Oxfam in 2018, 42 individuals owned as much wealth as 50 per cent of the global population, and this statistic is probably worse today. Good leaders can't ignore statistics like that and will love justice and want to see fairness and equality in the world. Bad leaders propagate inequality as it maintains the status quo, which has done very well for them, and their primary motivation is bettering themselves.

Personally, I have always had a keen sense of justice and have always hated the fact that the world is so imbalanced and unfair. Some of this comes from growing up in an affluent area on the edge of one of the largest public housing estates in the country, Wythenshawe, and being told as a child that it was those people's fault that their situation wasn't as good as mine, which I instinctively knew just wasn't true. I grew up with a strong sense of wanting to help create a more equal society, which is what led me to work in inner-city London for 13 years, trying to achieve just that. While we had some small wins, there were more failures and my work continues, with the themes of justice and equality running strongly through my business ventures.

The very well-known leaders throughout history such as Mother Teresa, Martin Luther-King, Mahatma Gandhi and Nelson Mandela are lauded and remembered precisely because they fought against injustice and achieved results against it. Two of these four paid for this with their lives, although you could argue a third, Nelson Mandela, also paid with a high percentage of his life, as he was incarcerated for 27 years. I believe most people are good and want more justice in our society, so what stops us being more active in fighting for justice with greater determination? As Desmond Tutu reminds us, to sit on the fence means to be on the side of the oppressor and to maintain the status quo. By default, too many of us have chosen the side of the oppressor and injustice by doing nothing. Why don't more of us act against injustice?

Part of the answer is simply because we are living from our conditioned self. We may have had a tough and humble background, so when we 'make it' to a better position in society, we tend to think to ourselves that we deserve it due to our hard work and skill. 'Why should we reverse some of what we have achieved by going backwards,' we think to ourselves. 'It's all down to us and our hard work, our children deserve better than we had it' and so forth. It is easy to justify those thoughts, but it is also dangerous to forget where we came from. To their credit, some successful entrepreneurs are fantastic at using their new positions to fight against injustice – whereas others tend to propagate it by doing nothing.

We live in an increasingly unequal world and that world now requires more leaders to risk their comfort and reputations to fight for those who don't have a voice to fight for themselves, and those who, in Rosa Parks's words, are 'tired of giving up'. A cause for the oppressed is helped enormously by those who are not suffering standing with them. In the civil rights movement in the fifties and sixties, many whites stood alongside their black brothers and sisters, and several were killed for their standpoint.

Another huge area of injustice is that of gender inequality. We need to have at least an equal number or, even better, more women on our leadership teams to redress the balance of hundreds of years of imbalance in the other direction. The feminine qualities of leadership are vital and need to be showcased to the world. I have been told by some that as a man I should leave talking about this subject to women, but I don't agree. The matter is so important that it needs both women and men to stand up for the injustice and misogyny shown against women in leadership.

Fighting for justice may mean losing some supporters and friends along the way, and others may perceive us to have tarnished our reputation, but if we know we are standing for justice and what is right, is that not that the most important factor? There is no doubt whatsoever that the Extinction Rebellion blockades in London in 2019 advanced the climate change debate considerably in the UK, yet many businesspeople who fully believed in the cause, including me, didn't take part because being arrested might not look good on our CVs or latest LinkedIn posts. Perhaps truly loving justice means that we sacrifice our reputation and our standing in society?

To truly stand up and to be passionate about seeing more justice does require some level of emotional engagement. There are those, often men, who need to develop in this area, and I am not sure we can really be lovers of justice until we 'feel' some of the pain that the oppressed feel and connect with the anger they feel towards their oppressors. The tragedy of climate degradation is another form of social injustice, as it is already impacting the poorer people of the earth long before it will have a material and financial impact on many in the West. Only this morning, I received an email from the community in Western Kenya, with whom our company is involved, telling us that yet again, extraordinary levels of flooding have occurred and, this time, for the first time, several of their cattle have been washed away. These freak weather conditions are now an annual occurrence due to climate change and have become far worse even in the ten years I have been involved.

I have already described becoming far more engaged in environmental issues after openly crying at a public event, when I shared a slide of people being made homeless through the impact of flooding due to climate change. Standing aside or remaining distant from people's troubles is impossible if you are going to be a leader who loves justice. Benjamin Franklin's quote is particularly apt here: 'Justice will not be served until those who are unaffected are as outraged as those who are.' The word 'outrage' sets the right tone and loving justice involves feeling anger and acting, not just talking about it. We will not see results overnight; it is a lifetime's work, but I, for one, do not want to be accused of being neutral in this increasingly unequal world.

Actions

Let's stand against injustice today:

» First, spend a few moments asking yourself how injustice for others makes you feel. Are you a little upset, or do you feel a stronger emotion that is prompting you to take action? Journal anything that comes to mind.

» You may well be aligned to a cause pertaining to justice already, but what are you personally doing to speak out or act for the oppressed in this situation?

» Thinking of your business or organisation, what more could you do, however small, to help reduce inequality whether that is within your company or organisation, local community or within your supply chain?

DAY 44 » **Honest**

Dictionary definition:

'Telling the truth or able to be trusted and not likely to steal, cheat or lie.'
Cambridge English Dictionary

Quotes:

'Honesty and transparency make you vulnerable. Be honest and transparent anyway.'
Mother Teresa, Albanian-Indian missionary

'Being honest may not get you a lot of friends but it'll always get you the right ones.'
John Lennon, English singer-songwriter

'Each time you are honest and conduct yourself with honesty, a success force will drive you toward greater success. Each time you lie, even with a little white lie, there are strong forces pushing you toward failure.'
Joseph Sugarman, American activist

'It's discouraging to think how many people are shocked by honesty and how few by deceit.'
Noël Coward, English playwright

Insights

I have a vivid memory of one day a long time ago, when I was working as a salesman for coffee and tea vending machines. The sales manager wanted us to end the quarter with some better numbers and wanted to encourage his team to sell at least another 20 contracts within the next week. We were all gathered in a room and told to contact potential customers with a story about Barclays Bank having cancelled an order, which meant we were able to do a special price on a certain model of vending machine. There were several more details than that in the story we were to spin, but absolutely none of them were true. After he had finished, I spoke up and said that I wasn't prepared to lie in order to sell more units, expecting others in the room to back me up, but no one else did. It was most definitely a tumbleweed moment! After the meeting, though, a few of my colleagues came to me and expressed their thanks for my honesty to which I thought, 'Thanks for your support during the meeting!' I have always had a thing about honesty, and it has led me into trouble on several occasions where I haven't been able to let dishonest people go unchallenged.

These days, I am perhaps more exercised than ever about the need for honesty in the business world, as it seems to be in short supply these days – even in companies that have admirable intentions in terms of their wider purposes. On more than one occasion, people working for well-known 'ethical' companies have made agreements at meetings in our offices and later reneged on them, even denying the conversations took place. I find this completely extraordinary: doing good in the world must surely extend to our honesty in our everyday business interactions? Despite many other failings from that era, I believe there needs to be a return to good old-fashioned Victorian honesty. In the British Parliament, it is forbidden to call one of your honourable friends a liar – yet lying is exactly what goes on a lot of the time. Even the politicians' PR machines are deemed to be given tacit permission to lie, although they have another word for it: spin. We are beset by 'fake news' and have accepted it as normal in the 21st century. Several years ago, the eventual winner of the BBC's TV show *The Apprentice* was found during the interview stages of the programme to have lied on his CV, but Lord Sugar still pronounced him the winner in the series finale the following week. Those lies were called out for what they were but renamed exaggerations, not lies. I wouldn't have employed him.

Another kind of dishonesty that is common is when people tell you what they think you want to hear, rather than what is the reality of the situation. I have experienced this on many occasions particularly when working in Africa, and it took me a few visits to be able to find techniques to cut to the truth. However, in our own Western culture, this kind of people-pleasing dishonesty is also commonplace. Other kinds of dishonesty occur when we omit essential details when sharing information, with the aim of presenting ourselves in a better light or when we market our companies to make them look better than they really are. Sometimes, if we repeat these stories enough, we almost come to believe in the new 'truth' we have fabricated around our lives and businesses. I know because I have done it too in the past, but an uncomfortable feeling rises in me these days until I correct myself. We have all observed children who, when they are not being completely honest, completely give themselves away with their body language. Almost all children do this as they have a pure conscience. If we keep ignoring our conscience as we grow older, we will soon start not to feel so uncomfortable when we are dishonest and then progress to not caring at all – so long as our dishonesty achieves our aims. Dishonesty can become the norm.

There is always a detectable aura of spin around us when we are not being truthful. If you are not a completely genuine or authentic person, or if there is something going on behind the scenes of a company, other people will often detect this through their intuition – even if they can't put their finger on exactly what it is. You know when you've had that uncomfortable, fuzzy feeling about someone who is trying to do some kind of business deal with you? I had that exact feeling with a Swedish drinks company we had just started dealing with as a distributor for the UK. They had a great backstory about their purpose, which was about how much good they were doing in the world and they made out that generating profit was very much a secondary concern. When I spent an afternoon in their offices asking them about the finer details and exactly how the farmers in the developing world were benefiting, they simply couldn't give me any hard facts and figures. I just couldn't get rid of that 'lack of openness' feeling I had about them for the rest of the day. During dinner that evening with their team, after a few glasses of wine had been consumed, their true colours came out and I went to bed that evening knowing that we weren't going to have a long-term business relationship with the company. Dishonesty and lack of transparency are much the same thing.

There is another reason to living a life that is super-honest and transparent: our own health. In an honesty experiment conducted by two University of Notre Dame professors, results showed that telling the truth is good for our health. 'Recent evidence indicates that Americans average about 11 lies per week. We wanted to find out if living more honestly can actually cause better health,' said lead author Anita E.

Kelly, PhD, professor of psychology at the University of Notre Dame. She continued, 'We found that the participants could purposefully and dramatically reduce their everyday lies, and that in turn was associated with significantly improved health.' Dishonesty seems to put barriers up between us and other people, both through their perception of us but also because our own confidence and ability to stand tall reduces when we are not completely honest. In the same study, we read: 'In weeks when participants told fewer lies, they reported that their close personal relationships had improved and that their social interactions overall had gone more smoothly that week.' It reveals: 'Statistical analyses showed that this improvement in relationships significantly accounted for the improvement in health that was associated with less lying.'

Often we excuse our 'white lies' on the grounds that they are designed to make us or our business seem better to others, but it does seem that this approach will likely achieve the opposite effect in the long term. Others will consciously and subconsciously like us more and do more business with us when we are open and honest, so let's live that way. Spin, lack of transparency, white lies, exaggerations are all part of dishonesty – and when we start to remove these from our lives, we will not only have better businesses and organisations but also improve our health.

Actions

Today, let's reflect on exactly how honest we are:

» I'm sure most readers of this book are honest people, but let's examine ourselves for a few moments. Are you always 100 per cent honest with others or do you occasionally exaggerate, slightly twist the truth or hide information that would be better out in the open?

» Imagine standing in a pool of light where all your secrets are exposed. Are there some secrets that it would be good to tell someone else confidentially? If so, decide to do that today.

» Metaphorically speaking, do you wear a work mask, or does the real, honest you shine through? Today, turn up your alertness and try to pick yourself up and correct yourself if you find you are not being 100 per cent honest.

DAY 45 » **Self-caring**

Dictionary definition:

'The act of caring for yourself when you are ill or to stop yourself
from becoming ill.'
Cambridge English Dictionary

Quotes:

'In dealing with those who are undergoing great suffering, if you feel
"burnout" setting in, if you feel demoralised and exhausted, it is best,
for the sake of everyone, to withdraw and restore yourself. The point
is to have a long-term perspective.'
Dalai Lama, Tibetan spiritual leader

'Our bodies are our gardens – our wills are our gardeners.'
William Shakespeare, English playwright and poet

'When you recover or discover something that nourishes your soul
and brings joy, care enough about yourself to make room for it in
your life.'
Jean Shinoda Bolen, American psychiatrist and author

'If we do not know how to take care of ourselves and to love ourselves,
we cannot take care of the people we love.'
Thich Nhat Hanh, Vietnamese Buddhist monk

Insights

Many of the characteristics we have been looking at over the course of this book relate to our outward behaviour towards others, or around those inner changes that are required for us to be better human beings. If we are not careful, though, we can become too frenetic in our self-improvement journey out of a desire to help others, which can apply too much pressure on ourselves. Without nurturing and caring for ourselves, we will lose the energy to carry on. Burnout is a common phenomenon amongst those who give themselves to others, whether in the caring professions or business; and many of us would do well to be kinder to ourselves in order to be able to give out more effectively. Notice that the dictionary definition of self-caring, above, is about preventing ourselves from becoming ill; the fact is that many of us have experienced ill health through not self-caring enough.

I spent several years living and working with a team in a poor urban community in southeast London. When some of the team moved to north London to start another project, a colleague and I decided to give ourselves a semi-sabbatical. We continued with scaled-down versions of some of our previous activities, but for at least three mornings a week, I sat alone in a church hall, reading, reflecting and noting my thoughts in a journal. I discovered a more contemplative part of myself, which had always existed but had been squeezed out by frenetic activity in trying to transform lives in the inner city. I had exhausted myself to the point of burnout; and that time and space proved essential for my starting to learn to look after myself.

Several years later, by now in the business world, I had to relearn the lesson, in a harsher way this time, when my business almost disappeared completely, with me running around like a headless chicken to try to save it. Several years later, I am in a much better place with a good balance of work, reading and writing (intellectual stimulation), relaxation and exercise. Keeping the balance between those four elements is the key to my self-care. I am now more attuned to my body and mind telling me when I am out of balance, through signals that I previously ignored for more than 20 years. If I had learned to listen a little earlier, I probably would have avoided a mild stroke a few years ago.

Knowing our own body is important, as is sensing when we are not in flow (Day 20), and at the peak of our performance. Corey McComb, an American musician and writer, puts this well in his article 'How to Maintain a State of Creative Flow': 'There is still a strong undercurrent in our society, particularly amongst entrepreneurs, that continues to celebrate and glamorize the grind. Just like with conversations around how much sleep is best to have each night, there is an unspoken competition around who can stay in the pressure cooker, working the longest and the hardest.' McComb quotes Ernest Hemingway, who said, 'I always worked until I had something done, and I always stopped when I knew what was going to happen next. That way I could be sure of going on the next day.' Stopping working when I am still performing well is still something I am learning, sometimes being a slave to my 'to do' list instead.

A good balance of stimulation and relaxation of both body and mind is a good way to think about self-care. If you have a physical job, then the body is exercised at work and I would recommend intellectual or creative stimulation as part of your self-care, such as reading or painting. Many more people have mentally stimulating jobs these days, but without any physical component, and they would do well to ensure they exercise during the week and at the weekend as part of their self-care. Relaxation too is important for both body and mind. For the mind, this may be enjoying a novel or watching a film; and for the body, it may mean a hot tub or massage. Sleep nourishes both body and mind (we talk on Day 12 about how our subconscious brain can operate and benefit us during sleep). Holidays are also incredibly important, as being away from our own domestic and work environment allows relaxation to happen on a far deeper level than when in our normal environment.

Now, you may be thinking that some of these nourishing activities cost money that you never seem to have enough of. It is true that neither holidays nor massages come cheap. I would see it as an important role of company leaders to ensure that they are paying everyone enough to have decent holidays and also giving them plenty of paid time off to be able to relax. At Cotswold Fayre, we don't allow people to carry holidays over or to get paid in lieu, as we believe that we are being a responsible employer by 'forcing' people to take plenty of time off. We also have a masseur come to the office from time to time! We have recently introduced work sabbaticals, which gives people even more time off every seven years. In fact, the word sabbatical comes from Sabbath and the ancient Jewish communities would not only have one day off a week and plenty of public holidays each year, but every seven years they would take the whole year off. Now, that's what I call self-caring!

What is it that stops us self-caring and being driven down the hyper-activity road so fast that we sometimes career out of control and off the road? Simply put, it is often not loving ourselves enough. Now, this isn't self-love in a narcissistic kind of way, but it's about knowing that you deserve that gorgeous meal out when travelling on business, or that you don't need to feel guilty about spending £80 on a massage because your body needs it. Looking after yourself means that you will be better able to give to others later in the week. Clearly there is a difference between self-care and self-indulgence: the latter leads to lethargy and inactivity rather than productivity. For example, allowing yourself to relax in front of a film for 90 minutes, after which you may feel more energised, can be very different to slumping in a front of a box set for five hours, after which you may feel less energised and probably guilty too. This is not to say that extended box sets are never right for anyone any time; one day, they may be just what you need to recharge yourself. The worse thing we can do in this area is to set up rules, as it is about knowing your own body and mind, and being disciplined about the food and nourishment you provide to both.

As the Dalai Lama says, self-care is about having a long-term perspective. We are here on this planet for a long time and hopefully have many years in which to create our legacy. Let's look after ourselves so we are still as effective and creative at 78 as we were at 28.

Actions

Today is about looking after yourself:

» Reflect on the four aspects of stimulation and relaxation for both body and mind (i.e. work, physical exercise, intellectual and creative stimulation, relaxation). Do you have these four in balance? Journal about your thoughts and ideas for change.

» For later this week, book a self-pampering session that you wouldn't normally book for yourself, for example a massage, face treatment or swim and sauna.

» As a leader, are you ensuring that those under your care enjoy good mental health by being able to relax their body and mind as necessary – and do you pay them enough for them to afford to do so? What are you doing in the workplace to help your people be creative and relax?

DAY 46 » **Friendly**

Dictionary definition:

'Characteristic of or befitting a friend; showing friendship.'
Dictionary.com

Quotes:

'Friendship is when your love for someone exceeds your need for them.'
> *Dalai Lama, Tibetan spiritual leader*

'Friendship... is born at the moment when one man says to another "What! You too? I thought that no one but myself..."'
> *C. S. Lewis, British author and theologian*

'There is a magnet in your heart that will attract true friends. That magnet is unselfishness, thinking of others first; when you learn to live for others, they will live for you.'
> *Paramahansa Yogananda, Indian monk and guru*

'Friendship is the hardest thing in the world to explain. It's not something you learn in school. But if you haven't learned the meaning of friendship, you really haven't learned anything.'
> *Muhammad Ali, American boxer and political activist*

Insights

By the word 'friendly' in this context, I am really talking about the ability to make good friends and to remaining in true friendship; 'knowing true friendship' is what we are discussing here. All great leaders and visionaries have had good friends, and I believe that we need these friends and they need us to make everyone's dreams happen. Consider this lovely definition of friendship from the Urban Dictionary:

> Friendship is when you love someone with every ounce of your being and genuinely want them to be happy even if it means sacrificing something yourself to make them happy. A true friend is someone you can talk to about your feelings, someone you can tell things you could never tell your family or even your partner. They are someone who you don't have to talk to but someone you want to talk to; someone you will go out of your way to be with. Friendship is when you love someone so much you want to hold them and never let go, someone you want to rest your head on and cry, and you would let them cry on you too. It's someone you can talk to about things you disagree on and end up being closer for that disagreement. It's when you think about someone and how close you are to them and how much you love them, and you smile and are happy all over.

While friendship is about nurturing relationships that sustain us and build us up, friendships only work if we are aiming to put in more love and support that we take out of them. I am sure we have all had so-called friendships that weren't like that at all but sucked us of energy; clearly that is not what we are talking about here. I love the C. S. Lewis quote, which beautifully indicates the initial common bond that may mark the beginnings of a true friendship. Lewis talks about friendship being about side-to-side love rather than erotic love, which is face to face. There is certainly a sense that friendships form due to a common interest or by achieving a common purpose; when we are side to side, we are facing outward rather than inward. In that way, whereas a lover's love would be challenged by someone else joining the relationship, friendship welcomes others to join in and is not jealous of others.

It does seem that true friendship is on the wane in the 21st century. The word 'friend' has been degraded by social media; someone connecting to you on social media is described as a friend but is probably not even a real acquaintance in many cases. Nor is it possible to have the huge number of friends that some people have as connections on social media. In the early 1990s, the anthropologist Dr Robin Dunbar concluded that humans could only maintain social relationships with an average of 148 people, which would include friends, family and less close acquaintances. His later research broke down this figure into different layers where the emotional closeness was considered. The layer closest to us has 3 to 5 people, the next layer has 15, the third layer has 50, and so on. Interestingly, I was asked recently to write down 50 people who had nourished me during my life, which I managed to do relatively quickly, but I know I would have struggled to write down very many more.

This research fits with the ancient mystics, who would have 12 to 15 disciples and often a closer group of 3 to 5 individuals within that number. We know from our own experience that it can be difficult to be very close to more than 3 or 5 people. The obvious question now is to ask ourselves whether we have these friendship layers in our lives today. Some have told me that they don't need close friends outside their relationship with their partner. Wrong, we all need friends outside our life partner relationships! Quite often these individuals will be of the opposite gender to your partner. You may sometimes need to talk about your relationship with your partner outside of it, and this isn't a display of disloyalty if the motivation is to be a better partner yourself.

Friendship is also often degraded by life and busyness. Often, the closest friendships we have are forged at formative times in our lives and these nurturing friendships can last a lifetime. Many of us, however, find that time for these friendships can become squeezed once we start having children, or perhaps geographical distance may also be a factor. Our philosophical or political points of view may diverge as we become older and we can realise one day that despite being in a good marriage or partnership, we sense an element of loneliness due to the lack of friendship. In my case, without necessarily realising it at the time, I 'lost' two of my closest friends around the time that my first marriage broke down. Understandably perhaps, they didn't want to stay close to me as they didn't want to upset my ex-wife. Later, I did try to reconnect with them both on more than one occasion, but neither seemed to be interested, which was painful at the time. However, rather than grieving for lost close relationships from the past, let's keep our eyes open for those friendships aligned with where we are now.

One thing I am sure of, though, is that we all need a deep and honest connection with someone on a similar journey to ourselves. Aristotle called this 'perfect friendship' or 'friendships of virtue'; and he believed that unlike accidental friendships formed through work and pleasure, which tended to be short-lasting and shallow, friendships of virtue require time and trust to build, and they depend on mutual growth. It is the life-giving sense of nourishment coming through these friendships that make them so essential and it is that depth of friendship that many of us crave more of as we become older.

Now that we have looked at the concept of friendship, hopefully you are feeling inspired to build more friendships of virtue into your own life; so all that remains is for you to become a good friend to others. How do we do this? First of all, it is about being as equal and open with the friend about yourself as they are with you. Not being afraid to hold your friend accountable or to challenge them when you have a different point of view is also important. At the same time, in a good friendship you absolutely accept your friend as they are and do not try to change them. You do not compete with them and you want the best for them, even if that means they beat you to a prize or something similar that you both want. Finally, you will always show up for a friend, whether in the middle of the night or if they need your help when they are a long way from home.

If you desire more friends, simply think of that magnet in our heart as described by Paramahansa Yogananda: this is the magnet of unselfishness, thinking of others first and learning to live for others. That way, friends will be attracted to you.

Actions

Discovering the art of true friendship can be time-consuming, but today:

» First, reflect on your friendships: are they nourishing you; are you nourishing them; how many good friendships do you have? Write them down and be thankful for those people.

» If you feel you do not have enough of these relationships, think of who you could approach for a glass of wine or a coffee in order to build a closer relationship. Ask yourself whether there are any relationships that aren't nourishing you and that you need to withdraw from.

» How can you be a better friend to others? Do you go the second mile when there is a friend in need? Do you want the best for your friends even when you may lose out as a result?

DAY 47 » **Calm**

Dictionary definition:

'Not disturbed, agitated or excited; under control.'
Collins English Dictionary

Quotes:

'Never be in a hurry; do everything quietly and in a calm spirit. Do not lose your inner peace for anything whatsoever, even if your whole world seems upset.'
St Francis de Sales, French bishop and saint

'Stay calm inside! You will then see that outside storms of life, even the most terrible ones, will turn into soft winds.'
Mehmet Murat Ildan, Turkish author

'When our mind is calm, we're better able to find peace of mind and live a joyful life.'
Dalai Lama, Tibetan spiritual leader

'One of the best lessons you can learn is to master how to remain calm.'
Catherine Pulsifer, Canadian businessperson and author

Insights

I remember hearing about a six-year-old whose parent apologised to him, saying: 'I'm sorry I shouted at you, honey; it's just that I am really under pressure right now.' The child responded: 'So being under pressure makes you yell at small children? I think you really have a problem...' Out of the mouths of babes comes great wisdom. The ability to stay calm under pressure is a sign of good leadership. This calm is not to be mistaken for a lack of emotions, but is a way for us to stay strong and available for people in a spirit of calmness, as there are plenty of opportunities for them to be brought into anxiety and panic elsewhere. How calm are you? Those go-getting type of people, who often become leaders, sometimes have a short fuse and may need to train themselves to stay calm or to bring some calm into their lives daily.

Richard Stengel tells us in his book *Mandela's Way* that the great man placed an enormous amount of importance on calmness, and relates that: 'I was once sitting next to Mandela in the back-seat of his armour-plated BMW, and his driver was lost. This was not unusual – his motorcade often went awry. The driver was accelerating and making screeching turns as if to make up for lost time. Mandela leaned forward and said to the fellow, "Let's be calm, man."' Stengel describes Mandela as hot-headed and easily roused before he went to prison, but he came out of prison the very opposite, calm and impossible to ruffle. Spending hours on his own in prison brought him a calmness that it would have been impossible for him to learn while constantly on the run from the authorities. And it is similar for us, I think. Most of us are constantly on the move, running around and being 'productive', and we don't stop for long enough to find that inner calm, which would help us find happiness and joy and to make better decisions.

In preparation for writing on being calm today, I reread the story of Chelsey Sullenberger, the pilot who landed his passenger plane on the Hudson River after a flock of geese had taken out both engines. It has now been made into the film *Sully*. Sullenberger and his co-pilot, Skiles, had 3 minutes, 32 seconds to make their decisions, while the plane was descending at a rate of a lift falling two floors every second. Incredibly, during this time, the co-pilot looked up the emergency procedures in the plane's quick-reference handbook! Imagine being in that situation and being calm enough to be thumbing through a handbook. Quite astonishing. As you will know, the landing was a success and Sully's first words to his co-pilot after the landing on the ice-cold water were, 'It wasn't as bad as we thought.' Clearly none of us are likely to find ourselves in that sort of situation, but I have always been intrigued to know how calm I would be in frightening circumstances like that.

But to bring us back to earth for a minute, we all experience various levels of stress during our working day and our times at home or travelling. How calm are we? Quite often things don't go according to plan, which leads to emotions of annoyance or sadness, so we attempt to control the situation and can end up even less calm, in a vicious circle. There was a first-century philosopher called Epictetus who in helping people find a level of calm, encouraged them to ask the question, 'What is out of our control?' When we do this, we find that most things in life are out of our control, but what are within our control are ourselves and our reaction to what is going on around us. We are rarely in full control of everything around us, but we are in control of how we respond to it. Epictetus said, 'When we are frustrated, angry or unhappy, never hold anyone except ourselves – that is, our judgments, accountable.'

One of the benefits of meditation or periods of quiet during our day is to learn to be calm. In fact, one of the many meditation apps around now is called exactly that: 'Calm'. I'm sure that learning to still our mind at the start of each day helps us maintain that calmness throughout the day. Yet it is so difficult sometimes to still our minds. We are either thinking about what happened earlier that day or the day before, or thinking about what we must achieve in the coming day. We can end up focusing on anything but being in the present moment, and I'm convinced that learning to live in the present moment is what helps us develop inner calm more than anything else. A common technique is to breathe deeply and focus the mind on the breath and the breath alone. When your mind wanders, don't castigate yourself, but just bring the mind back to the breath and focus all your mind on that breath as you breathe in deeply and breathe out slowly. As mentioned, there are various apps around that can help you learn the process and it becomes easier after a few weeks of regular practice. Mindfulness is very on trend these days, but there are more people talking about it than actually learning the discipline of meditating to the extent that it will really impact our life and brings calm and peace into our lives and leadership.

It is to Winston Churchill that the phrase 'Keep calm and carry on' is attributed and two million posters of his now ubiquitous slogan were printed in 1939 as preparations began for war. They were to be used if and when the Germans invaded the UK, and as that never happened, the posters were never seen by the public – until Stuart Manley unearthed one when sorting through a box of old books in Northumberland in 2000. There is something Churchill-like, though, about that calm, bulldog determination of persevering in adversity. I love the phrase 'calm determination', as it takes us away from the zen-like state some people may imagine in relation to the words 'meditation' and 'calm': we can be people of action and perform great exploits yet have a wonderful sense of calmness about us. That is probably the main difference between my younger self and the Paul Hargreaves of today. My younger self was all about doing and there wasn't much calm for me or others around me. Now I am much calmer and am learning to 'be'; I do less than before but achieve more, although I still have much to learn about being calm. Ask yourself now: would other people describe you as calm? Every day? Or just on a good day?

Actions

Today keep calm and carry on:

» But first, set your phone timer for eight minutes and sit in calm. Focus on the repetition of each breath, as described above, and bring yourself back to the breath when your mind wanders.

» Reflect upon how calm you are in your day-to-day life. Remember that we can only control ourselves, often not the events around us. When you find yourself stressing and worrying today, take a short 'time out' to remember that truth.

» During the day, when you remember, take a few deep breaths and focus on the present moment. One way of doing this is to set alarms on your phone.

DAY 48 » **Persevering**

Dictionary definition:

'Determined to continue to do or to try to achieve something, despite problems.'
Cambridge English Dictionary

Quotes:

'No one succeeds without effort... Those who succeed owe their success to perseverance.'
Ramana Maharshi, Indian sage

'Life is not easy for any of us. But what of that? We must have perseverance and above all confidence in ourselves. We must believe that we are gifted for something, and that this thing, at whatever cost, must be attained.'
Marie Curie, Polish physicist and chemist

'Look at a stone cutter hammering away at his rock, perhaps a hundred times without as much as a crack showing in it. Yet at the hundred-and-first blow it will split in two, and I know it was not the last blow that did it, but all that had gone before.'
Jacob August Riis, Danish-American social reformer

'Success depends upon staying power. The reason for failure in most cases is lack of perseverance.'
J. R. Miller, American pastor

Insights

The Growthink website shares the story of the difficulties that J. K. Rowling experienced before publishing her first Harry Potter book. Most people know about her amazing success and wealth today, but it is good to remember the perseverance it took her at the beginning – which should inspire us all. Rowling had her first book rejected by 12 different publishers, including her eventual publisher, Bloomsbury, who told her to 'get a day job'. Rowling describes her life as being a complete mess at the time, as she was going through a divorce and living in a small flat with her daughter while writing, as well as being recently bereaved of her mother. How easy it would have been to give up, but her perseverance kept her going and now the Harry Potter brand is worth $25 billion.

And there are countless other stories like that of household names who have achieved well beyond their dreams in the arts, business or charities despite a discouraging start. Yet it is easy to look at them and think, 'I wish I had had their luck, or just happened to be in the right place at the right time.' Yes, there is always a large degree of luck – as many entrepreneurs and YouTube sensations would tell you – but what others don't see are the years and years of hard work and perseverance that came before the success. I was going to include 'diligent' as one of these 50 characteristics in this book, which can be defined as 'works hard in a careful and thorough way' according to the Collins English Dictionary; but 'diligent' felt like too safe a word, and most of us who are leaders would already have plenty of diligence. Where we can grow and stretch ourselves is in perseverance, and the word 'perseverance' has within it a sense of pursuit of an impossible dream or achieving something against the odds in a way that those who are only diligent will never achieve. Of course, significant achievements will always require huge amounts of dedication, hard work and attention to detail, but perseverance means continuing to pursue your dreams, despite setbacks and what others may say.

In fact, while anything I have achieved is clearly nowhere near that of Rowling, I too was told by an older businessperson to go and get a proper job when I was starting the company, just like J. K. was told by her publisher. Perseverance carries with it some stubbornness and 'bloody-mindedness' as they would call it in Yorkshire and a sense of 'don't you go telling me what I should be doing'. Now, stubbornness must be tempered by humility and sometimes it is right to be guided by others and change course. But if we are to follow our dreams, then we will need to persevere to achieve them, despite what others may say. Consider Jacob August Riis's quote above, with his image of the stonecutter hammering away for a hundred blows before anything happens. Would we give up after 20, 30, 50, 80, 99 blows? Those who turned up to watch a few seconds before the final blow that broke the stone would think, 'That was easy work, I could do that.' But they haven't seen the hard work before, every blow of which contributed. And we can be taken in like that too sometimes, seeing the short period before the launch of a product or business without seeing the years or decades of graft and perseverance that came before.

We looked at resilience on Day 27, which is about the ability to bounce back from setbacks, but perseverance for me is more about the consistent hard work, sometimes boring work, with our eyes fixed on our dreams. In the early days of the business, I put in some crazy hours, mainly doing boring tasks such as picking customers' orders in the warehouse after everyone else had gone home. It was tedious, dull, unskilled work, but necessary to achieve the dream of being the primary supplier of fantastic speciality food to independent retailers all over the country. I didn't particularly enjoy being in the warehouse until midnight, it certainly wasn't fun, but I had my eyes on the goal and pushed through so that now I am privileged to do what I choose to do. The next dream, which has already taken two years to come to fruition, is building a food hall and kitchen, which, as I write, the builders have nearly completed and is due to finally open six weeks after this book is published. Again, lots of perseverance was required by me and the others involved, but the artist's impression of the finished building kept us going through the long planning process.

Most people have dreams when they are younger, yet too many of us give up on them. I am in my fifties and still pursuing some of mine. So, what is it that crowds into our mind and stops us from pushing on until our dreams are fulfilled? For some it is a confidence issue; they have been told too many times they can't do it and start to believe what others say, and then give up completely or compromise by doing something that their heart is not set on. We have done a great disservice to our young people through the disintegration of family and community in the Western world, reducing the likelihood of them having a crowd of supportive people around them. For others, financial hardship or children (the two may be connected) force them into doing a job that takes them away from their dreams but is perceived as a safer option due to having a larger income. Sometimes it is right to put our dreams on hold, yet still persevere inside until we can fire up again later, perhaps with a better financial safety net. Let us not let financial pressure lead to mediocrity, though.

I lived in Oxfordshire for a while in my thirties, where I seemed to be surrounded by people of a similar age, many of whom had given up on their dreams from their younger days and were now only focusing on working towards their pensions. I found it quite sad and wanted to fire them up again and help them dream their forgotten dreams, so that they would start taking actions to make them come true. In fact, this is often what happens during the classic mid-life crisis, when people who once had big dreams of changing the world arrive at 40-something and realise they are halfway through their lives and haven't achieved what they dreamed of when younger.

So, assuming we don't want to be like them, how can we build more perseverance into our lives, so we don't give up but persevere until we achieve our goal? We have talked about risk-taking and not being afraid of failure. Understanding from the beginning that things will always go wrong and preparing yourself to push through when that happens are also important. You won't achieve everything overnight, so set mini goals and then celebrate them when they are achieved. Having people to support you who are not immediately connected to your goals can be very helpful. Finally, while you may be wholly focused on your purpose and it may be tempting to 'work, work, work', that isn't always the most productive way, so ensure that you have plenty of leisure time and exercise too. Just imagine if J. K. Rowling had given up her dream after the 12th rejection. Let's not give up.

Actions

Learning to build more perseverance into our lives:

» Ask yourself whether you have given up on your dreams in the past or more recently, whether large and small. Reflect for a few moments and ask why and what has stopped you. Journal about your thoughts.

» To what extent do you have a support network to help you persevere, or could you be part of that network for anyone else?

» Are there any dreams that have been left to one side that you could start planning to resurrect today? The risk now perhaps may not seem as large as it once was.

DAY 49 » **Authentic**

Dictionary definition:

'Representing one's true nature or beliefs; true to oneself or to the person identified.'
Dictionary.com

Quotes:

'The inner voice has both gentleness and clarity. So to get to authenticity, you really keep going down to the bone, to the honesty, and the inevitability of something.'
Meredith Monk, American composer and director

'Authenticity is about imperfection. And authenticity is a very human quality. To be authentic is to be at peace with your imperfections... Great leaders don't see themselves as great; they see themselves as human.'
Simon Sinek, British-American author and motivational speaker

'Authenticity is the alignment of head, mouth, heart, and feet – thinking, saying, feeling, and doing the same thing – consistently. This builds trust, and followers love leaders they can trust.'
Lance Secretan, Canadian businessman and author

'Hard times arouse an instinctive desire for authenticity.'
Coco Chanel, French fashion designer and businesswoman

Insights

The word 'authentic' tends to be overused in the 21st century with respect to leaders, so I hesitated to include it here; but, on consideration, it makes for a good word on the penultimate day of our reflections. Those lacking in all the other characteristics we have looked at – compassion, humility, kindness, etc. – will not be authentic, as there will inevitably be a certain amount of acting and falseness in their interactions with others. Those who struggle to know their purpose, are unavailable to others and always feel dissatisfied, are lacking in authenticity too. That's not to say that life is a bed of roses for authentic individuals; there are most definitely struggles, but, to me, the word 'authentic' carries with it a sense of the real and an inkling of being able to see more deeply into someone than a person's exterior; a meeting with a person's soul or heart or essence, whatever you want to call it.

I was inspired to write the daily meditations in this book by two things: first, the lack of my own authenticity I have seen around me in leaders over the years, and, second, a sense in which I realised I had gradually grown into a level of authenticity through several so-called negative experiences, and recognising this marked a transition from the very inauthentic place I was in when I was younger. My management team and I have engaged with an organisation called 'Being at Full Potential' and one of their courses is called 'Stepping into Authentic Leadership'; and, of course, there is a connection between authenticity and leadership as realising our full potential both as human beings and leaders is impossible without authenticity. Some of the ancient wisdom that fuels this organisation's excellent courses comes from the Hindu gurus of India; ancient wisdom is often the best, and much of what is often introduced in the 21st century as being new is in fact based on rediscovering old ways. Ancient wisdom would always say that coming through trials and tribulations is the best way of forming the real person and developing authenticity.

Last night, I happened to see part of a TV programme called *The Real Marigold Hotel*, about a bunch of older celebrities who spend a month in India to investigate whether they could retire there, although most of them probably had no intention of doing so! There was one beautiful scene towards the end of their time there when two of the celebrities went to an ashram and met the local guru. There was a moment when the guru held their hands for a while, looked into their eyes and said, 'Welcome home.' Both the celebrities were moved to tears and didn't really know why. It was clear to me that was a genuine encounter with real authenticity; those two heartfelt words were enough. So let's explore and understand a little more about what it means to be truly authentic.

The Latin root of the word 'authentic' means author. So, it is about more than being honest, full of integrity and genuine – it is about being the author of your own life. There is a blank page waiting to be written on by our lives and authenticity comes from us writing on that blank sheet from our heart. The trouble is that we are born into an imperfect world and can sometimes come to that page in early adulthood, when we find the page is no longer blank and has felt-tip scribbles drawn on it by others as we grew up. These can be other people's expectations, false promises, unrealistic targets, disappointments and the like. Some of these scribblings can be difficult to erase in order for us to write our own story, and we may need help from others in order to do so. After we have restored the blank sheet, we can face another challenge: the feeling that we should write what others want written there. 'Should' is a terrible word and should be banned. Oops! There can be an expectation for us to conform to cultural and social norms without being free to express exactly who we are; it is not much different to having a straitjacket put on us.

We may have heard many times from others that we simply need to be ourselves, and that is what authenticity is about; but it can take us a while to discover who we really are. Even when we have only just started on the journey of self-exploration, it is that authentic self of ours that people will connect with, trust and respect. They can finally see us for who we really are, the cloak has been removed. Dr Nina Burrows is the author of *The Little Book of Authenticity* and in an article in the *Guardian,* in 2014, she wrote: 'Embracing your authenticity is the only way to become "you" and being "you" is the greatest asset you have when it comes to being a leader. It's your "self" that others will be inspired by, connect with and ultimately trust. It's your "self" that they will follow.' After all, it is quite difficult to be someone else, but many of us still try – or maybe we don't try, but spend our lives wishing we were another person. It is incredibly exciting to realise you are unique and the story to be written on that blank piece of paper can only be written by you as your authentic self.

That is not to say that the story won't change over time; that would be both unrealistic and inauthentic too. Our story grows and evolves. Sometimes, politicians can attract a lot of negativity when they switch parties or change their views on what they are fighting for over the years. I don't have a problem with this, as there is often a higher degree of authenticity on those occasions than in staying within a party whose policies they had diverged from. They may have struggled to fit in with their old party because both they and possibly the party have changed over the years. Being authentic can be about evolution. Bob Dylan constantly reinvented himself in a musical sense, and many of his fans gave him a lot of criticism when he entered his 'electric phase', for example. Dylan seems to have been an authentic guy on a musical journey, not pandering to the tastes and expectations of his fans. Compare him to some other artists who churn out the same old stuff, as they know it will pull the crowds in and keep their record label happy.

Being authentic is about being aware of our weaknesses and imperfections and not covering them up. It is about knowing that whatever we have achieved may be largely due to luck or being in the right place at the right time. Most of all authenticity is about truly knowing our humanity and enjoying simply being ourselves.

Actions

To step into authenticity today:

» To what extent do you wear any masks or cloaks that prevent people from seeing the real you? Do you cover anything over? Reflect for a few minutes and journal about any thoughts.

» Consider that blank page of your life and think about it for a few moments. Are there any scribblings on there from others that need rubbing out? Any expectations, any 'shoulds'?

» Today, if you find yourself 'acting', try to pause, step back and come back to being the real you.

DAY 50 » **Good**

Dictionary definition:

'1. having admirable, pleasing, superior, or positive qualities; not negative, bad, or mediocre.
2. morally excellent or admirable; virtuous; righteous.'
    Collins English Dictionary

Quotes:

'Do your little bit of good where you are; it's those little bits of good put together that overwhelm the world.'
    Desmond Tutu, South African cleric and theologian

'Do all the good you can. By all the means you can. In all the ways you can. In all the places you can. At all the times you can. To all the people you can. As long as ever you can.'
    John Wesley, English cleric and theologian

'Be good to people. You will be remembered more for your kindness than any level of success you could possibly attain.'
    Mandy Hale, American author and speaker

'I'm a good person. In most ways. But I'm beginning to think that being a good person in most ways doesn't count for anything very much, if you're a bad person in one way.'
    Nick Hornby, English writer and lyricist

Insights

So, we come to the final day of our reflections on the characteristics of a leader and end up with the broadest characteristic yet: 'good'. For the dictionary definitions today, I have used two different aspects of good – but what does it mean to be described as a 'good' leader? What is goodness? I used the term in the title of my previous book, *Forces for Good*, but I didn't actually define the word 'good', assuming that most of us have a general sense of what is good for other people and good for the planet. Utilitarianism is the philosophy of the greatest good for the greatest number, but to achieve that goal, one could potentially be bad to a minority of people, so I'm not sure this approach captures the essence of the characteristic I want to talk about here.

A friend suggested that another definition of good may be to be working continually towards achieving the United Nations Sustainable Development Goals (SDGs) throughout the world. In our company's latest impact report, we have flagged which aspects of what we do count towards the different SDGs. This is a small way in which we are good as a company. Increasingly, this is how businesses will be judged. Undoubtedly, if every business leader in the world became more collaborative, humbler, more loving and so on all – working their way through all our 49 other characteristics – then they would also become a better person, would lead a better business and the world would be a better place. So maybe on our last day, our emphasis could be to focus on those aspects of our character where we need to improve – that'll be all of them in my case!

To take a different perspective, in Nick Hornby's novel *How to be Good*, written from the perspective of a wife, Katie, we follow the transformation of her husband, David, a cynical man who writes a newspaper column called 'The Angriest Man in Holloway', in which he rants and raves about anyone different to himself. In the early part of the book, Katie has had enough and wants a divorce but decides she should try to make the marriage work because she is a 'good person'. The question of what it means to be good is at the heart of this story. David's character is impacted by the arrival of a faith healer called DJ GoodNews, who manages to encourage David to replace his life of cynicism with an unquestioning, all-embracing love of mankind. David goes on to write self-help books for others, encourages his children to give their toys to the poor and asks GoodNews to move in with them. So, David becomes everything Katie wanted him to be, yet she finds this very difficult, preferring the old David, and this challenges her own perceptions of what 'good' is.

There are, I suppose, three types of people and leaders who may read this book (discounting those who know they are not good and who don't want to change, but they wouldn't have bought the book). First, there are people like David, who know they are not good but are going through the process of change. Second, people like Katie, who previously thought they were quite good but are now are being challenged as to whether they are good or not. And finally, those in the middle, who are developing in some areas but also keenly aware that they still need to grow in others. More likely, we will feel part of all three groups on different days. On some days, I am very aware of my lack of goodness and that my mistakes seem larger than ever, but I try not to be hung up on those and move on with more awareness so as not to make the same errors again in the future. On other days, I feel like I am good, but will then have an encounter in which I am challenged and inspired by others to be better. And on other days, I am more aware that I seem to be flowing and growing with a sense of purpose.

In order to progress, we will find ourselves gradually becoming more aware of our weaknesses, challenged and encouraged, or possibly all three at the same time. Certainly, it is important not to castigate yourself if you feel you are not making progress in your journey of becoming a good leader. You may on occasions feel like you are going backwards in order to move forwards. That's absolutely fine and probably demonstrates progress anyway, as you become more self-aware, so do please be gentle on yourself. To become a better leader is a lifetime's work, and it may take a long time before we see development and we may also need to face certain experiences to mould us. That is all I am really asking you to do: to be open to being moulded rather than fighting against adversity. Something else to remember is that it is impossible to work all this out in your head. We can certainly decide to be more vulnerable, for example, but we can't make it happen with just the intellectual part of our brains. Change involves our emotions and the other non-thinking parts of our brain, which we can't turn on at will. The key is to be open and spend time with others whom you admire and who inspire you.

How to be good, or at least how to be better, does require, first of all, deciding and then planning to commit to this path. Hopefully some of the actions I have given you on each day will help here, as you will certainly make progress as you practise them. Think of three Ps: plan, practise, progress. As leaders, we can make a huge difference globally by increasing our love for others and the world. What we do may seem insignificant or tiny, but added together and with many more people doing their part too, our combined actions will make a significant difference to this broken world. Let's finish with the words of Desmond Tutu: 'Do your little bit of good where you are; it's those little bits of good put together that overwhelm the world.'

Actions

How to be good today?

» Plan: what are you going to do today to be a better leader? Make a shortlist on a fresh page and add to it over the coming days.

» Practice: put in place the means of practising new ways of being a leader that are easy enough to do every day.

» Progress: ask to be accountable to someone else whom you respect and let them monitor your progress. Learn from the wisdom and goodness of others.

Bibliography

Self-aware

Eurich, T. (2018). *Insight: The Power of Self-Awareness in a Self-Deluded World*. London: Pan.

Ferriss, T. (2020). *The Tim Ferriss Show* with guest Brené Brown. Available at: https://tim.blog/2020/02/06/brene-brown-striving-self-acceptance-saving-marriages/ Accessed: 1/06/June 2020.

Waite, T. (1996). *Footfalls in Memory*. London: Coronet.

Wignall, N. (2018). '5 Habits of Highly Self-Aware People.' Available at: https://medium.com/personal-growth/5-habits-of-highly-self-aware-people-8e0799986e16 Accessed: 1/06/2020.

Wong, K. (2017). 'A Beginner's Guide to Self-Awareness.' Available at: https://medium.com/the-cut/a-beginners-guide-to-self-awareness-be8eb7a8da54 Accessed: 1/06/2020.

Humble

Lewis, C. S. (2012). *Mere Christianity*. London: Collins.

Ravindran, S. (2014). *The Being Leader*. YOU-Nity Project Academy.

Forgiving

Mandela, N. (1995). *Long Walk to Freedom*. London: Abacus.

Stengel, R. (2010). *Mandela's Way*. New York: Crown.

Empathetic

Gentry, A., Todd, J. and Sadri, G. (2016). 'Empathy in the Workplace – A Tool for Effective Leadership.' Available at: https://cclinnovation.org/wp-content/uploads/2020/03/empathyintheworkplace.pdf. Accessed: 15/04/2020.

Malik, N. (2019). 'With Respect: how Jacinda Ardern showed the world what a leader should be.' *Guardian*. Available at: www.theguardian.com/world/2019/mar/28/with-respect-how-jacinda-ardern-showed-the-world-what-a-leader-should-be . Accessed 1/05/2020.

Gracious

Raz, G. 'How I built this'. Weekly podcast by NPR (USA). Available at: www.npr.org/podcasts/510313/how-i-built-this?t=1609423183897. Each week Guy Raz interviews an entrepreneur; comments in this chapter are based on listening to around 100 of his podcasts from 2018–2020.

Solitary

Waite, T. (2016). *Taken on Trust*. London: Hodder & Stoughton.
— (2020) 'Terry Waite: What my years in captivity taught me about coping with isolation.' *Daily Telegraph*. Available at: www.telegraph.co.uk/men/thinking-man/terry-waite-years-captivity-taught-coping-isolation Accessed: 1/05/2020.

Playful

Lindley, P. (2017). *Little Wins.* London: Penguin.

Servant-like

Sinek, S. (2017). *Leaders Eat Last*. London: Penguin.
Devasahayam, M. (2016). 'Mother Teresa a true servant-leader'. *Straits Times*. Available at: www.straitstimes.com/asia/south-asia/mother-teresa-a-true-servant-leader-the-statesman-columnist Accessed: 15/04/2020.

Thankful

Emmons, R. A. (2008). *Thanks!* New York: Mariner Books.

Kind

Alden, L. and Trew, J. (2012). 'If it makes you happy: engaging in kind acts increases positive affect in socially anxious individuals.' Available at: https://pubmed.ncbi.nlm.nih.gov/22642341/ Accessed: 1/06/2020.

Forster, K. (2017). 'Manchester attack: How people showed kindness and bravery in the face of unspeakable terror.' *Independent*. Available at: www.independent.co.uk/news/uk/home-news/manchester-attack-bombing-acts-of-kindness-terrorism-cabs-homes-help-free-taxis-homeless-mancunians-a7751886.html Accessed: 1/05/2020.

Proctor, M. (2020). '6 Science-Backed Ways Being Kind is Good for your Health.' Available at: www.quietrev.com/6-science-backed-ways-being-kind-is-good-for-your-health Accessed: 1/06/ 2020.

Zaki, J. (2016). 'Kindness Contagion: Witnessing kindness inspires kindness, causing it to spread like a virus.' *Scientific American*. Available at: www.scientificamerican.com/article/kindness-contagion Accessed: 1/06/2020.

Generous

Ferrero, B. (2018). 'Circle of Joy.' Available at: www.thesacredbraid.com/2018/04/10/tuesdays-with-story-41018 Accessed: 15/04/2020.

Creative

Hemingway, E. (1994). *A Moveable Feast*. London: Arrow.

Teller, A. (2016). 'The unexpected benefit of celebrating failure.' TED talk. Available at: www.youtube.com/watch?v=2t13Rq4oc7A Accessed: 15/04/2020.

Content

Figueres, C. and Rivett-Carnac, T. (2020). *The Future We Choose*. London: Manilla Press.

Compassionate

The Dalai Lama (2002). *An Open Heart*. London: Hodder.

Kerry (2011). 'Difference Between Empathy and Compassion.' Available at: www.differencebetween.net/language/difference-between-empathy-and-compassion/#ixzz6O1SU4D7H Accessed: 1/05/2020.

Courageous

The Wizard of Oz (1939). Directed by Victor Fleming and adapted from *The Wonderful Wizard of Oz* by L. Frank Baum (1900).

Self-sacrificial

Jake, R. (ed). (2020). '7 Truly Inspiring Stories of Self-sacrifice.' Available at: www.ba-bamail.com/content.aspx?emailid=31597 Accessed 1/07/2020.

Joyful

Hargreaves, P. (2019). *Forces for Good*. Bristol: SRA Books.

Vulnerable

Windwood, A. (2013). 'No More Experts.' Available at: http://interactioninstitute.org/no-more-experts/ Accessed: 15/04/2020.

Integrous

Esplin, B. (2017). '5 Inspiring stories of people who value integrity more than money.' Available at: http://micawberprinciple.com/5-inspiring-stories-of-people-who-value-integrity-more-than-money-1794/ Accessed: 1/07/2020.

Flowing

Carson, C. (ed). (2000). *The Autobiography of Martin Luther King*. London: Abacus.

Inclusive

Cassella, N. (2017). 'What Peter the Great Realized About Inclusivity.' Available at: https://civicskunk.works/what-peter-the-great-realized-about-inclusivity-810cd5c30cac Accessed: 1/06/2020.
Wilkinson, R. and Pickett, K. (2010). *The Spirit Level*. London: Penguin.

Anonymous

Freiberg, K. and Frieberg, J. (2019). '20 Reasons Why Herb Kelleher Was One of the Most Beloved Leaders of Our Time.' *Forbes* Magazine. Available at: www.forbes.com/sites/kevinandjackiefreiberg/2019/01/04/20-reasons-why-herb-kelleher-was-one-of-the-most-beloved-leaders-of-our-time Accessed: 1/05/2020.

Available

Matthews, D. (2019). 'Why Active Listening is the Most Foundational Leadership Skill.' Available at: https://medium.com/better-marketing/why-active-listening-is-the-most-foundational-leadership-skill-e14bccfb19dc Accessed: 1/05/2020.

Murdock, R. (2020). 'Radical Availability.' Available at: http://robertfmurdock.github.io/2020/03/20/RadicalAvailability.html Accessed: 1/05/2020.

Patient

Morris, M. (2018). 'How Success is Like a Chinese Bamboo Tree.' Available at: www.mattmorris.com/how-success-is-like-a-chinese-bamboo-tree Accessed: 1/06/2020.

Hospitable

Meyer, D. (2010). *Setting the Table*. London: Marshall Cavendish.

Silent

Cumming, L. (2018). 'Experiencing the silent walk for Grenfell.' Available at: https://www.quaker.org.uk/blog/experiencing-the-silent-walk-for-grenfell Accessed: 1/05/2020.

Dix, M. (2015). 'Four Lessons I learned from Silence.' Available at: https://aboutmeditation.com/power-of-silence/ Accessed: 1/05/2020.

Resilient

Nietzsche, F. (1888) *Twilight of the Idols.*

Collaborative

Heffernan, M. (2012). 'Why Mergers Fail.' CBS News. Available at: www.cbsnews.com/news/why-mergers-fail/ Accessed: 15/04/2020.

Koulopoulos, T. (2015). '5 of the Most Surprising Statistics about Startups.' Available at: www.inc.com/thomas-koulopoulos/5-of-the-most-surprising-statistics-about-start-ups Accessed: 15/04/2020.

Poole, E. (2014). '7 Deadly Sins – capitalism's flat-earth problem and what to do about it.' JustShare lecture at St Mary Le Bow, 29 January 2014. Available at: http://evepoole.com/7-deadly-sins-capitalisms-flat-earth-problem/ Accessed: 15/04/2020.

Sinek, S. (2019). *The Infinite Game*. London: Penguin.

Interdependent

Perry, J. (2017). 'I Accuse Individualism.' Available at: https://bthechange.com/i-accuse-individualism-2a538d318bf6 Accessed: 15/04/2020.

Purposeful

Oppong, T. (2017). 'The Dangerous Approach of Living Without Purpose.' Available at: https://medium.com/personal-growth/the-dangerous-approach-of-living-without-purpose-798a87c5d3a6 Accessed: 1/06/2020.

Connected

Moore, C. (2010). 'No Such Thing as Society: a good time to ask what Margaret Thatcher really meant.' *Daily Telegraph*. Available at: www.telegraph.co.uk/comment/columnists/charlesmoore/8027552/No-Such-Thing-as-Society-a-good-time-to-ask-what-Margaret-Thatcher-really-meant Accessed: 1/07/2020.

Peace-loving

'Nonviolence.' Standford University: The Martin Luther King, Jr. Research and Education Institute. Available at: https://kinginstitute.stanford.edu/encyclopedia/nonviolence Accessed: 1/07/2020.

Gentle

Saʿdī (2012). *The Gulistan, Or, Flower-Garden.* Memphis: General Books LLC.

Curious

Lindley, P. (2017). *Little Wins*. London: Penguin.

Contrite

Frizzell, K. (2014). 'The Power of Apologizing: Why Saying "Sorry" IS So Important.' Available at: https://tinybuddha.com/blog/power-apologizing-saying-sorry-important/ Accessed: 1/07/2020.

Protective

Pangelinan, D. (2017). '3 Steps to Develop a Protective Leadership Mindset.' Available at: https://magazine.vunela.com/3-steps-to-develop-a-protective-leadership-mindset-bf47eadd8d2e Accessed: 1/06/2020.

Intuitive

Borreli, L. (2013). 'Can an Organ Transplant Change a Recipient's Personality? Cell Memory Theory Affirms "Yes".' *Medical Daily*. Available at: www.medicaldaily.com/can-organ-transplant-change-recipients-personality-cell-memory-theory-affirms-yes-247498 Accessed: 1/05/2020.

Martone, R. (2011). 'The Neuroscience of the Gut.' *Scientific American*. Available at: www.scientificamerican.com/article/the-neuroscience-of-gut Accessed: 1/05/2020.

Ruder, D. (2020). 'The Gut & the Brain.' Available at: https://neuro.hms.harvard.edu/harvard-mahoney-neuroscience-institute/brain-newsletter/and-brain/gut-and-brain Accessed: 1/05/2020.

Non-judgmental

Sol, M. (2017). '13 Signs You're a Judgmental Person (and How to End the Habit).' Available at: https://lonerwolf.com/judgmental-person/ Accessed: 1/05/2020.

Self-disciplined

Tyrrell, M. (2011). 'Self-discipline and Mental Health.' Available at: www.uncommon-knowledge.co.uk/self-discipline Accessed: 1/06/2020.

Wise

Barlament, J. (2019). 'Distinguishing between Knowledge, Intelligence, and Wisdom.' Available at: https://medium.com/@jwbarlament/distinguishing-between-knowledge-intelligence-and-wisdom-e8d-7f244477f Accessed: 1/07/2020.

Loving

Cuellar, T. (2018). 'Leading With Love: An Unconventional Approach to Leadership.' *Forbes*. Available at: www.forbes.com/sites/forbescoachescouncil/2018/06/29/leading-with-love-an-unconventional-approach-to-leadership/#70723cf11123 Accessed: 1/06/2020.

Lewis, C. S. (2016). *The Four Loves*. London: Collins.

Stallard, M. (2020). 'Is There a Place for Love in Leadership.' Available at: www.michaelleestallard.com/is-there-a-place-for-love-in-leadership Accessed: 1/06/2020.

Justice-loving

Carson, C. (ed). (2000). *The Autobiography of Martin Luther King*. London: Abacus.

Rosa Parks biography (2018). Available at: www.biography.com/activist/rosa-parks Accessed: 1/07/2020.

Honest

Kelly, A. (2012). 'Lying Less Linked to Better Health, New Research Finds.' American Psychological Association. Available at: www.apa.org/news/press/releases/2012/08/lying-less Accessed: 1/07/2020.

Self-caring

McComb, C. (2018). 'How to Maintain a State of Creative "Flow".' Available at: https://medium.com/s/story/how-to-master-the-flow-state-one-simple-yet-difficult-trick-56854fca9109 Accessed: 1/05/2020.

Friendly

Allan, P. (2018). 'This is How Many Friends You Need to Be Happy.' Available at: https://lifehacker.com/this-is-how-many-friends-you-need-to-be-happy-1823425885 Accessed: 1/05/2020.

Lewis, C. S. (2016). *The Four Loves*. London: Collins.

Ulmo (2008). Urban Dictionary definition of friendship. Available at: www.urbandictionary.com/define.php?term=Friendship Accessed: 1/05/2020.

Calm

Gambardella, S. (2019). 'Epictetus: The Calm Switch.' Available at: https://medium.com/the-sophist/epictetus-the-calm-switch-ebfed-fb760cc Accessed: 1/06/2020.

Stengel, R. (2018). *Mandela's Way*. New York: Crown.

Persevering

Lavinsky, D. '7 Entrepreneurs Whose Perseverance Will Inspire You.' Available at: www.growthink.com/content/7-entrepreneurs-whose-perseverance-will-inspire-you Accessed: 1/06/2020.

Syed, M. (2011). *Bounce*. London: Fourth Estate.

Young Entrepreneurs Council (2019). '9 Ways You Can Improve Your Perseverance Skills.' Available at: www.success.com/9-ways-to-improve-your-perseverance-skills Accessed: 1/06/2020.

Authentic

Burrowes, N. (2014). 'Think authenticity is about being honest and open? Think again.' *Guardian.* Available at: www.theguardian.com/women-in-leadership/2014/apr/11/real-meaning-authenticity-leadership# Accessed: 1/07/2020.

Good

Hornby, N. (2014). *How to be Good*. London: Penguin.

Acknowledgements

First, I wish to thank all those leaders who have inspired me over the years – some of you may know who you are, others may not.

I would also like to thank my team at Cotswold Fayre, who continue to inspire me every day: you are all so much better at what you do than I would be. I have always maintained that I only really have one talent and that is finding excellent people to work for me.

I am particularly indebted to Sujith Ravindran, who as well as leading what was a formative spiritual walk for me in 2018 and helping me appreciate the depth and beauty of Eastern spirituality, was also kind enough to write the inspiring foreword for this book.

Thank you also to the wonderful mix of creativity, philosophy, business and spirituality that is known as Host – many of you have been formative to my thoughts in these pages.

The first Covid lockdown of 2020, with all its cancelled meetings and trips, allowed me time to write this book, but I am painfully aware that the virus took many loved ones with it – my heart goes out to all those who lost loved ones during the pandemic in 2020–21.

The pandemic, though, was also a wake-up call to many of us to engage in our local communities and I am grateful for the inspiration and friendship of those in my own village of Latton – you know who you are!

This book wouldn't be what it is without the excellent team at SRA Books, who also published my first book. Your ideas and suggestions are always better than mine. In particular, thanks to Sue Lascelles, Andrew Chapman, Paul East and Sue Richardson.

To all those I lead, either directly or indirectly, thank you for allowing me to get leadership wrong, and thank you for those who often tell me where I can improve. I look forward to the adventures we have planned for the next few years.

Finally, thanks again to my long-suffering wife, Nicola, who endured hours of solitude of her own at home while I was researching and writing this book.

About the Author

Paul Hargreaves is one of the leading voices in the UK inspiring business leaders to move away from focusing on the single bottom line of profit, which only benefits shareholders, and encouraging them to work instead for the benefit of all stakeholders. More businesses are now realising that benefiting people and the planet is going to be essential for business success post Covid-19. Through  his books and speaking to other business leaders, Paul also inspires profound personal change – something he calls 'the fourth bottom line' – resulting in leaders with greater compassion and empathy for others. Paul's first book, *Forces for Good*, was favourably reviewed by *Management Today*, *Director Magazine* and *HR Director*, and in 2020 won a bronze award in the coveted USA-based Axiom Business Book Awards.

In 1999, Paul founded Cotswold Fayre, a speciality food wholesaler, while he was working for charitable organisations in a neglected community in southeast London. The company grew rapidly and is now the leading retail wholesaler of speciality food and drink in the UK, supplying over 1,800 retail sites within the UK from its office and warehouse in the Thames Valley. The tremendous success of the company has been down to creating a great place to work and being centred on changing the world for the better rather than profit alone. The company sells and distributes the highest quality food products, massively reduces carbon in the supply chain, has a strong community focus, and for the past decade has worked with a poor rural community in Western Kenya. Since 2015, Cotswold Fayre has been certified as a B Corporation. B Corps are companies that meet the highest standards of social and environmental performance, and Paul is also an ambassador for the movement within the UK. His role in the world of B Corps and his first book have led to him becoming a seasoned speaker, helping other businesses that want to change their culture for the better.

Paul has four adult children and lives with his wife, Nicola, in the Cotswolds.